WHERE?

ERIN McHUGH

Sterling Publishing Co., Inc.
New York

Library of Congress Cataloging-in-Publication Data Available

10   9   8   7   6   5   4   3   2   1

Published by Sterling Publishing Co., Inc.
387 Park Avenue South, New York, NY 10016
© 2005 by Erin McHugh
Distributed in Canada by Sterling Publishing
^{c}/o Canadian Manda Group, 165 Dufferin Street
Toronto, Ontario, Canada M6K 3H6
Distributed in Great Britain by Chrysalis Books Group PLC
The Chrysalis Building, Bramley Road, London W10 6SP, England
Distributed in Australia by Capricorn Link (Australia) Pty. Ltd.
P.O. Box 704, Windsor, NSW 2756, Australia

Sterling ISBN 1-4027-2572-8

For information about custom editions, special sales, premium and
corporate purchases, please contact Sterling Special Sales
Department at 800-805-5489 or specialsales@sterlingpub.com.

WHERE?

ROAD TRIP

The first paved road was seven-and-a-half miles long and six feet wide and was built in Egypt. Made from slabs of sandstone, limestone, basalt, and pieces of petrified wood, experts believe it dates back 4,600 years to the time the great pyramids were built. Ancient Egyptians used the road to transport basalt blocks from the stone quarry to a nearby lake. The blocks were then floated across the lake, which connected to the Nile, where they traveled to a site in Giza.

◆

LETHAL INJECTION

Southern Africa is home to the fastest snake alive—the black mamba, an extremely aggressive reptile that can reach top speeds of up to twelve miles per hour. It moves along flat land with the front third of its body elevated as high as four feet off the ground, which makes it easier to move rapidly. Animals that fall prey to the black mamba die within minutes; a human might last up to four hours. No matter who or what gets bitten, the fatality rate is close to 100 percent.

◆

YEOW!

The United States Postal Service reports that postmen really do get bitten by dogs with some regularity, at a rate of over 3,000 chomps—and at a cost of over $25 million to the USPS—each year. The best advice for postal carriers is either to avoid or transfer out of the Metropolitan Los Angeles area, known as the "Dog Bite Capital" to the cognoscenti.

"WHERE SHALL FREEDOM RING?"
From Dr. Martin Luther King Jr.'s "I Have a Dream" speech

"And if America is to be a great nation this must become true. And so let freedom ring from the prodigious hilltops of New Hampshire. Let freedom ring from the mighty mountains of New York. Let freedom ring from the heightening Alleghenies of Pennsylvania!

"Let freedom ring from the snowcapped Rockies of Colorado! Let freedom ring from the curvaceous slopes of California!

"But not only that; let freedom ring from Stone Mountain of Georgia!

"Let freedom ring from Lookout Mountain of Tennessee!

"Let freedom ring from every hill and molehill of Mississippi. From every mountainside, let freedom ring.

"And when this happens, when we allow freedom to ring, when we let it ring from every village and every hamlet, from every state and every city, we will be able to speed up that day when all of God's children, black men and white men, Jews and Gentiles, Protestants and Catholics, will be able to join hands and sing in the words of the old Negro spiritual, 'Free at last! Free at last! Thank God Almighty, we are free at last!'"

◆

HONOLULU hosts the only royal palace in the United States. The Iolani Palace, built in 1882 by the last king of Hawaii, King David Kalakaua, remained a royal residence until the monarchy was overthrown in 1893—though it served as capitol of the provisional government, republic, territory, and state of Hawaii until 1969. It is now a museum.

LONG DIVISION

A continental divide is a ridge or elevated area that directs the flow of water running into adjacent drainage basins.

- **North America** is one of the only continents with two divides. The Western Continental Divide, often called the Great Divide, runs from British Columbia into the United States along the Rockies, continuing southward into Mexico and Central America. The Eastern Continental Divide runs through the Appalachian Mountains, separating land draining east to the Atlantic Ocean from land to the west, draining to the Mississippi River and Gulf of Mexico.
- **South America** is split by the Andes Mountains, which run nearly the full length of South America, divide land draining west into the Pacific Ocean and east toward the Atlantic.
- **Australia** has fairly indistinct water and mountain boundaries and is surrounded by water, making it difficult to define a single divide.
- **Europe** and **Asia**'s continental divides are equally difficult to distinguish because they both contain a number of large bodies of water into which rain falls and drains, including the North, Black and Baltic Seas, and the Arctic and Atlantic Oceans.

WHERE'S THE GAME?

In May 1874 the first intercollegiate football game under American rules (not soccer or rugby) was played: Harvard vs. McGill in Cambridge, Massachusetts. Home team ruled.

LONG MAY SHE WAVE

According to Presidential Proclamation, or in some cases, U.S. law, the American flag is always displayed at the following locations:

Mount Slover limestone quarry, in Colton, California, by act of Congress. The first flag was raised on July 4, 1917.

Fort McHenry National Monument and Historic Shrine, in Baltimore, Maryland, by Presidential Proclamation, July 2, 1948.

Flag House Square, Albemarle and Pratt Streets in Baltimore, by public law approved March 26, 1954.

United States Marine Corps Memorial (Iwo Jima), Arlington, Virginia, by Presidential Proclamation, June 12, 1961.

Lexington, Massachusetts, Town Green, by public law approved November 8, 1965.

The White House by Presidential Proclamation, September 4, 1970.

The Washington Monument displays fifty U.S. flags around its perimeter; by Presidential Proclamation, July 6, 1971.

United States Customs Service at ports of entry that are continuously open; Presidential Proclamation, May 5, 1972.

National Memorial Arch, Valley Forge State Park, Valley Forge, Pennsylvania, by public law approved July 4, 1975.

In addition, the American flag is presumed to be on continuous display on the surface of Earth's Moon, having been placed there by the astronauts of *Apollo 11*. The first flag was replaced because the force of *Apollo 11*'s return to lunar orbit knocked the flag down.

FORECAST: DRY

Antarctica is the world's largest desert, covering over 5.5 million square miles. Deserts are generally described as an arid region that either receives less than ten inches of rain per year or where the potential evaporation rate is twice as great as the precipitation. The world's largest deserts:

Desert	Square Miles	Rainfall/Year (inches)	Temp (°F)
Antarctica	5,500,000+	<2	-129–58+
Sahara	3,500,000+	< 5	55–135+
Arabian	1,000,000+	4–20	30–129+
Gobi	500,000	<2.7–8	40–113+

LESS—AND MORE—THAN ZERO

The equator is at 0 degrees latitude and is 24,901.55 miles long. The Tropic of Cancer and the Tropic of Capricorn each lie at 23.5 degrees latitude—the Tropic of Cancer is located at 23.5° north of the equator and Tropic of Capricorn lies at 23.5° south.

Brazil is the only country that passes through both the equator and a tropic. The word *tropics* is most commonly used to describe the area bound by the Tropic of Cancer on the north and Tropic of Capricorn on the south.

◆

ISRAEL is ineligible to sit in on the United Nations Security Council because it is the only member nation that is not a member of any regional UN grouping.

TINY TERRITORY
The 10 smallest countries in the world...

Country	Land Mass/ Location	Type of Government
Vatican City	0.17 sq. mi. Holy See, Rome, Italy	Pope has executive power
Monaco	0.75 sq. mi. French Mediterranean, near Nice, France	Constitutional monarchy
Nauru	8.2 sq. mi. Pacific island	Republic
Tuvalu	10 sq. mi. Nine small islands scattered in Western Pacific	Constitutional monarchy with parliamentary democracy
San Marino	24 sq. mi. Surrounded by Italy	Republic
Liechtenstein	62 sq. mi. Between Austria and Switzerland	Hereditary constitutional monarchy
Marshall Islands	70 sq. mi. North Pacific	Constitutional government in free association with the U.S.
St. Kitts and Nevis	104 sq. mi. Caribbean Sea	Constitutional monarchy

Country	Land Mass/ Location	Type of Government
Seychelles	107 sq. mi. Indian Ocean	Socialist multiparty republic
Maldives	115 sq. mi. Indian Ocean	Republic

◆

"EVERY MAN A REMBRANDT!"

This was the promise from the team that created one of the biggest fads of the 1950s: paint-by-numbers. Its invention is attributed to Max S. Klein, owner of the Palmer Paint Company of Detroit, Michigan, and his partner, artist Dan Robbins, who also conceived the idea and actually designed many of the early paintings. The first kits appeared in 1951 under the CraftMaster name, and by 1954 it had become a full-blown craze, with twelve million kits sold.

Robbins said the idea had come to him from something a high school teacher had mentioned: Michelangelo often mapped out portions of a work-in-progress (including the Sistine Chapel), numbering the parts so he could remember the colors later. Robbins proposed abstract art for the debut kit, as was the fashion of the day, but America's new *artistes* preferred landscapes, seascapes, animals, and, yes, clowns.

◆

BOSTON LIGHT was the first lighthouse in America, and the last one to be automated.

WHERE'S THE WINNER?

There's a long-standing argument about the world's longest place name. Here are the choices:

Llanfairpwllgwyngyllgogerychwyrndrobwllllantysiliogogogoch

This Welsh town's name means "Saint Mary's Church in the hollow of white hazel near a rapid whirlpool and the Church of Saint Tysilio near the red cave." Though often called simply Llanfair PG, natives point out that the railway station, which opened in 1848, has a fifteen-foot sign sporting all 58 letters.

Tetaumatawhakatangihangakoauaotamateaurehaeaturipukapi-
himaungahoronuku pokaiwhenuaakitanarahu (92 letters)

This is a hill on New Zealand's South Island. The name is said to mean "the place where Tamatea, the man with the big knees, who slid, climbed, and swallowed mountains, known as land eater, played his flute to his loved one." This is featured as the world's longest place name in *The Guinness Book of World Records*, but Welsh proponents say it's not commercially used, and is, after all, only a hill.

And Thailand has entered the fray with the 167-letter "poetic name" of Bangkok:

Krung thep mahanakhon bovorn ratanakosin
mahintharayutthaya mahadilok pop noparatratchathani
buriromudomratchanivetmahasathan amornpiman
avatarnsathit sakkathattiyavisnukarmprasit

This is considered by many to be an unfair addition to the

contest, as it is more of a lengthy description of Bangkok from a loving resident's eye, and is not in popular use; most often it is abbreviated to Krung Thep, or "City of Angels." The translation is:

The land of angels, the great city of
immortality, various of devine gems,
the great angelic land unconquerable,
land of nine noble gems, the royal city, the pleasant capital,
place of the grand royal palace,
forever land of angels and reincarnated spirits,
predestined and created by the highest devas.

◆

WHO ARE YOU CALLIN' YANKEE?

Astronomer Charles Mason and surveyor Jeremiah Dixon were hired by the British courts to settle a property dispute in the colonies about two pieces of land: one which Charles I of England had given to Lord Baltimore, and the other that Charles II had gifted to William Penn. From 1763 through 1767, the surveyors undertook this enormous feat, and finally the Mason-Dixon Line was defined as the boundary between Pennsylvania and Maryland running between latitude 39°43'26.3"N and latitude 39°43'17.6"N. The survey was completed to the western limit of Maryland in 1773; in 1779 the line was extended to mark the southern boundary of Pennsylvania with Virginia (now West Virginia). It was only during debates over the Missouri Compromise in 1820 that Congress began to popularize the Mason-Dixon Line as the boundary dividing "free states" from "slave states." Today it remains a colloquialism for dividing the North from the South.

A WORLD OF ITS OWN
Where everything isn't as it should be . . . or is it?

Bizarro World is a place populated by accidental, imperfect duplicates of Superman, Lois Lane, and their friends. Back in a 1959 edition of DC Comics, Superman's archenemy Lex Luthor botched an experiment with a duplicator ray, producing a chiseled, chalk-faced version of Superman. Complete with superpowers, he was not evil, but due to his lack of intelligence, he was somewhat dangerous. Feeling rejected, Bizarro, as he was called, moved to his own planet, Htrae, which is shaped like a cube and is, of course, the word Earth spelled backward. Superman constructed an ugly, chalk-faced Bizarro Lois mate for him, and Bizarro used an "ancient advanced technology" to populate his planet with countless replicas of himself and his lady love. They lived according to the strict, backward Bizarro Code:

Us do the opposite of all Earthly things!
Us hate beauty! Us love ugliness! Is a big crime to make
anything perfect on Bizarro World!

U.S. AIR BASES AROUND THE WORLD

U.S. military establishments can be found in these cities:

Aviano, Italy
Incirlik, Turkey
Kadena, Japan
Kunsan, South Korea
Lajes, Azores
Lakenheath, United
  Kingdom

Mildenhall, United Kingdom
Misawa, Japan
Osan, South Korea
Ramstein, Germany
Spangdahlem, Germany
Yokota, Japan

PASSION ON STAGE

The original and most famous Passion play began in the
Bavarian Alps in Oberammergau as a promise to God in 1633.
The townspeople were besieged by both the Thirty Years'
War and plague, and swore an oath that they would perform
the "Play of the Suffering, Death and Resurrection of Our
Lord Jesus Christ" every ten years. The following year they
began to fulfill that pledge—in a nearby cemetery surrounded
by the graves of plague victims. In 2000, the Oberammergauers
performed the Passion play for the fortieth time. Passion plays
have become increasingly popular over the years; other large
productions currently staged around the world include those
in Iztapalapa, Mexico; Eureka Springs, Arkansas; and
Canada's Badlands, in Alberta.

◆

THE TRAVELS OF TARZAN

Edgar Rice Burroughs's jungle hero really got around. Here
are some of the fictional spots where Tarzan swung in his
twenty-five novels, which have subsequently been translated
into more then fifty languages:

Ashair
Castra Sanguinarius & Castrum Mare
London-on-Thames
Opar
Pellucidar
Pal-ul-Don
Xujan Kingdom

THE SHINBONE'S CONNECTED TO . . .

A typical adult human skeleton consists of these 206 bones:

Axial skeleton

SKULL (22)
Cranial bones (8)
- frontal bone (1)
- parietal bone (2)
- temporal bone (2)
- occipital bone (1)
- sphenoid bone (1)
- ethmoid bone (1)

Facial bones (14)
- zygomatic bone (2)
- superior and inferior maxilla (2)
- nasal bone (2)
- palatine bone (2)
- lacrimal bone (2)
- vomer bone (1)
- inferior nasal conchae (2)
- mandible (1)

Middle ear bones (6)
- malleus (2)
- incus (2)
- stapes (2)

Throat (1)
- hyoid bone (1)

Vertebral column (26)
- cervical vertebrae (7) incl. atlas & axis
- lumbar vertebrae (5)
- thoracic vertebrae (12)
- sacrum (1)
- coccyx (1)

Thoracic cage (25)
- sternum (1)
- ribs (2 x 12)

Appendicular skeleton

Pectoral girdle (4)
- clavicle or collarbone (2)
- scapula or shoulder blade (2)

Pelvic girdle (2)
- coxal bone (2)

Upper limbs (60)
- humerus (2)
- radius (2)
- ulna (2)
- carpal (16)
- metacarpal bones (10)
- phalanx (28)

Lower limbs (60)
- femur (2)
- tibia (2)
- fibula (2)
- patella (2)
- tarsal (14)
- metatarsal (10)
- phalanx (28)

The infant skeleton has the following additional bones:

Sacral vertebrae (4 or 5), which fuse in adults to form the sacrum

Coccygeal vertebrae (3 to 5), which fuse in adults to form the coccyx

Ilium, ischium, and pubis, which fuse in adults to form the pelvic girdle

To recap:

- Skull and upper jaw (21 bones)
- Tiny ear bones, 3 each (6 bones)
- Lower jaw, or mandible (1 bone)
- Front neck bone, or hyoid (1 bone)
- Backbone or spine (26 bones or vertebrae)
- Ribs, 12 pairs—same for men and women (24 bones)
- Breastbone (1 bone)
- Each upper limb has 32 bones: 2 in shoulder, 3 in arm, 8 in wrist, 19 in hand and fingers (64 bones)
- Each lower limb has 31 bones: 1 in hip (one side of pelvis), 4 in leg, 7 in ankle, 19 in foot and toes (62 bones)

Total = 206 bones

FOREST LAWN RESIDENTS

One of the world's most famous cemeteries is where some of Hollywood's greatest were laid to rest; the Glendale location is the hillside where D. W. Griffith filmed *The Birth of a Nation* in 1915.

Forest Lawn—Glendale

Gracie Allen
L. Frank Baum
Wallace Beery
Humphrey Bogart
William ("Hopalong
Cassidy") Boyd
Joe E. Brown
George Burns
Jack Carson
Lon Chaney
Nat King Cole
Sam Cooke
Robert Cummings
Dan Dailey
Sammy Davis Jr.
Dorothy Dandridge
Walt Disney
Theodore Dreiser
Marie Dressler
W. C. Fields
Larry Fine
Errol Flynn
Clark Gable
Sid Grauman
Sydney Greenstreet

Jean Harlow
Jean Hersholt
Edward Everett Horton
Ted Knight
Alan Ladd
Louis L'Amour
Carole Lombard
Chico Marx
Aimee Semple McPherson
Tom Mix
Jack Oakie
Mary Pickford
Dick Powell
Norma Shearer
Red Skelton
Casey Stengel
Jimmy Stewart
Robert Taylor
Irving Thalberg
Spencer Tracy
Ethel Waters
Mary Wells
Ed Wynn
Robert Young

Forest Lawn—Hollywood Hills

Steve Allen
Gene Autry
Lucille Ball
Albert "Cubby" Broccoli
Bette Davis
Andy Gibb
Rick James
Buster Keaton
Charles Laughton

Stan Laurel
Liberace
Ozzie, Harriet, and
Ricky Nelson
Freddie Prinze
George Raft
John Ritter
Isabel Sanford
Telly Savalas

◆

MONDO MONOLITH

Uluru is the Australian Aboriginal word for "great pebble." Also called Ayers Rock, it is the world's biggest monolith. Made of arkose, a course-grained sandstone, it rises 1,043 feet above the ground, with a circumference of nearly five miles, and extends down over 3½ miles beneath the surface.

'TWAS NOTHING TO SNEEZE AT

Though Clement C. Moore's 1822 "A Visit from St. Nicholas" seems to take place in the country, he could have been describing his New York City home. Moore lived in a mansion on a huge estate, stretching from 18th to 24th Streets between Eighth and Tenth Avenues, in a Manhattan neighborhood now called Chelsea.

WHERE COUNTRIES GET HELP

Much of the generosity of countries around the world comes from money donated by member nations of the Organization for Economic Cooperation and Development to developing countries. The thirty funding democracies of the Organization for Economic Cooperation and Development work together to address the economic, social, environmental, and governance challenges of the world economy. Exchanges between OECD governments flow from information and analysis provided by the Secretariat in Paris. The Secretariat collects data, monitors trends, forecasts economic developments, and researches social changes. Each member country's contribution to the OECD annual budget is based on a formula related to the size of each member's economy. The budget for 2005 is 327 million euros (over 412 million U.S. dollars).

Country by rank	Contribution (%)
1. United States	24.975
2. Japan	23.128
3. Germany	9.467
4. United Kingdom	6.885
5. France	6.382
6. Italy	5.182
7. Canada	3.181
8. Spain	2.771
9. Mexico	1.996
10. Korea	1.932
11. Netherlands	1.876
12. Australia	1.736
13. Switzerland	1.454
14. Belgium	1.165

Country by rank	Contribution (%)
15. Sweden	1.083
16. Austria	0.926
17. Norway	0.784
18. Denmark	0.747
19. Turkey	0.706
20. Poland	0.651
21. Finland	0.583
22. Greece	0.546
23. Portugal	0.495
24. Ireland	0.399
25. Czech Republic	0.238
26. New Zealand	0.231
27. Hungary	0.181
28. Iceland	0.100
29. Luxembourg	0.100
30. Slovak Republic	0.100

◆

STROLL DOWN SEÑOR WENCES WAY

He was one of the most beloved acts on TV's *The Ed Sullivan Show*. A little man with a thick Spanish accent born Wenceslao Moreno, he was a ventriloquist without a dummy—he used his fist, a pen, and a little lipstick to make his character come alive. And when Señor Wences died just days after his 103rd birthday, New York City applauded him one more time, naming 54th Street between Sixth and Seventh Avenues "Señor Wences Way."

◆

PAJAMAS, a word that has a mysterious, luxurious sound, is from the Persian, *pa* (leg) and *jamah* (garment).

NO TRESPASSING

Schoolchildren in Massachusetts like to show off at being able
to pronounce the name of a local lake (which is also the
longest name for a lake in the United States):

Chargoggagoggmanchauggagoggchaubunagungamaugg

UNDERWATER VACANCY

At the bottom of Emerald Lagoon in Florida's Key Largo
Undersea Park lies Jules' Undersea Lodge, an authentic
underwater research lab that is also a hotel to scuba divers. In
deference to the protected environment, the entire structure
sits on five-foot legs. Guests trade Florida's renowned sunsets
for its interior, filled with compressed air, two bedrooms
(complete with sheets sporting an underwater theme), air
conditioning, TV, and all the usual amenities of aboveground
living, complete with gorgeous porthole undersea views. This
unusual hostelry takes its name, of course, from the world's
first science-fiction writer, Jules Verne.

BAD ADDRESS

A really bad place to live is 323 E. 107 Street in New York
City—so bad that when Black Hand leader Ignatius "Lupo
the Wolf" Lupo lived at the former horse lodgings in the early
1900s, it was called "The Murder Stable." Apparently Lupo
didn't even bother to dump the victims he whacked: Reports
were that when the place was finally demolished, the dead
had been buried right there, underneath the stable.

WHERE GULLIVER TRAVELED

The strange lands and less-than-perfect societies Lemuel Gulliver visited in Jonathan Swift's 1726 novel, Gulliver's Travels

Balnibarbi:	The island below Laputa, where things are done contrary to their natural order
Brobdingnag:	A country of giants whose views and culture mock those of eighteenth-century Europe
Glubbdubdrib:	An island of sorcerers and magicians, who are served by people from beyond the grave
Laputa:	A flying island of brilliantly scientific, yet extremely impractical, people
Lilliput and Blefuscu:	An island where everything is half the size (Lilliput) and its neighbor (Blefuscu) have an ongoing, pointless war about which end of eggs should be broken
Luggnagg:	A land of prideful yet polite and generous people, and home to the Struldbrugs, a small tribe of immortal people
Land of the Houyhnhnms and Yahoos:	Where intelligent horses rule over primitive, base humans

BILLED GATES

As final plans were laid in place for Central Park, architect Frederick Law Olmsted and landscape architect Calvert Vaux met opposition about their idea to make some of the park entrances special. New York City's café society suggested ornate gates for grand entrances in their carriages, which was anathema to the architects, prompting Olmsted to declare that "an iron railing always means thieves outside or bedlam inside." In 1862, the architects persuaded the park's commissioners to carve names into the stone walls near many of the entrances—or gates—instead. The commissioners chose the types of people and professions that they thought would most be enjoying the park. Clockwise, from Columbus Circle:

Merchants' Gate:	Columbus Circle
Women's Gate:	Central Park West at West 72nd Street
Explorers' Gate:	Central Park West at West 77th Street
Hunters' Gate:	Central Park West at West 81st Street
Mariners' Gate:	Central Park West at West 85th Street
All Saints' Gate:	Central Park West at West 97th Street
Boys' Gate:	Central Park West at West 100th Street
Strangers' Gate:	Central Park West at West 106th Street
Warriors' Gate:	Central Park North at Adam Clayton Powell Blvd. (Seventh Avenue)
Farmers' Gate:	Central Park North at Malcolm X Blvd. (Lenox Ave.)
Pioneers' Gate:	Duke Ellington/James Frawley Circle at Fifth Avenue
Vanderbilt Gate:	Fifth Avenue at East 106th Street
Girls' Gate:	Fifth Avenue at East 102nd Street
Woodmen's Gate:	Fifth Avenue at East 96th Street
Engineers' Gate:	Fifth Avenue at East 90th Street

Inventors' Gate:	Fifth Avenue at East 72nd Street
Scholars' Gate:	Fifth Avenue at East 60th Street
Artists' Gate:	Central Park South at 6th Avenue
Artisans' Gate:	Central Park South at 7th Avenue

◆

OTHER OSCARS
*Awards in other countries comparable to the
United States' Academy Awards:*

Canada: Genie
France: César
Great Britain: British Academy Film Award, the "BAFTA"
Italy: David di Donatello
Mexico: Ariel
Spain: Goya
Sweden: Guldbagge ("Golden Ram")
Taiwan: Golden Horse

HE YAM WHERE HE YAM

Popeye pops up as town mascot in three places in the United
States: There are oversized statues of the sailor man in Alma,
Arkansas, and Crystal City, Texas (Crystal City has two).
Alma and Crystal City have had a rivalry since the 1980s,
when each laid claim to the title "Spinach Capital of the
World." Both have Spinach Festivals, and Alma is also home
to Popeye Brand Spinach. Yet Zavala County's Crystal City
has billed itself "Spinach Capital" since 1937, having been
one of the nation's premier spinach growers since the 1920s.
But perhaps Popeye himself would feel most at home in
Chester, Illinois, birthplace of Popeye creator Elzie Segar.

WHERE DID THAT SONG COME FROM?
Odd stories and legends about some of our favorite tunes

"Kid Charlemagne" by Steely Dan: All about Stanley Owsley III, a major presence in the early Haight-Ashbury scene in San Francisco, and the first "underground" chemist to mass-produce high-quality LSD in the 1960s.

"California Dreamin'" by the Mamas and the Papas: John and Michelle Phillips wrote this on a cold night in New York City when Michelle was longing to be back in California.

"Big in Japan" by Alphaville: Many rock bands, like many Hollywood stars, find they continue to be "big in Japan" long after they cannot draw a large audience in the U.S. and U.K.

"Billie Jean" by Michael Jackson: Jackson wrote this song about a woman who used to stalk him and write him letters about a son she claimed was his.

"The House of the Rising Sun" by the Animals: An homage to a brothel in New Orleans that took its name from its proprietor, Madame Marianne LeSoleil Levant (hence, the "Rising Sun" moniker). Open from 1862 to 1874, it was located at 826-830 St. Louis Street. Leadbelly wrote the lyrics for this tune in 1945. The song was first recorded in the 1920s by Texas Alexander, then by other artists.

"Carry That Weight" by the Beatles: Paul McCartney wrote this about his struggle to keep the Beatles together after Brian Epstein's death from a sleeping pill overdose in 1967. It is recorded as one song with "Golden Slumbers" as part of a suite of unfinished songs at the end of *Abbey Road*.

"Cold Blooded" by Rick James: Written by the performer about his scary girlfriend of the moment, Linda Blair, who starred in *The Exorcist*.

"Lola" by the Kinks: Band member Ray Davies wrote this number after their manager got drunk at a club and started dancing with a transvestite he mistook for a woman. Toward the end of the night, "Lola's" stubble began to show, but by then the manager was too far gone to notice, or apparently care.

"Mama Told Me Not to Come" by Three Dog Night: Randy Newman wrote this about a party that was a little bit wilder than he expected; the drug scene was fairly new to American middle-class youth at that time.

"Pass the Dutchie" by Musical Youth: Originally the song was titled "Pass the Kutchie," meaning a marijuana pipe, but because all the band members were minors, the group's manager demanded a slight lyrical change.

"Philadelphia Freedom" by Elton John: A huge rugby fan himself, Elton dedicated this to friend and tennis star Billie Jean King, who coached the burgeoning World TeamTennis team from Pennsylvania called the Philadelphia Freedoms.

◆

YUMMY

The human tongue detects only four fundamental tastes—or a combination thereof: sweet, sour, salty, and bitter. The taste buds that are sensitive to salt are spread evenly over the tongue. Sweet tastes are experienced at the tip of the tongue, sour flavors on each side, and bitter ones toward the back.

DANTE'S NINE CIRCLES OF HELL

The Divine Comedy (1308–1321), Dante Alighieri's great epic poem, takes the reader through Dante's Inferno:

Circle 1: Limbo—unbaptized yet virtuous pagans

Circle 2: The Lustful—those overcome by carnal desires

Circle 3: The Gluttonous—overindulgers and obsessive consumers

Circle 4: Hoarders and Spendthrifts—the greedy, hoarders, and indulgers

Circle 5: The Wrathful—the gloomy who can find no joy

Circle 6: Heretics—religious dissenters

Circle 7: The Violent—those who commit sins against people and property, suicides, blasphemers, sodomites, and usurers

Circle 8: The Fraudulent—those guilty of deliberate evil: panderers, seducers, flatterers, false prophets, sorcerers, corrupt politicians, thieves, perjurers, counterfeiters, impersonators

Circle 9: Traitors—betrayers, either to relatives, country, guests, or lord; Satan himself resides in the Ninth Circle

TALK ABOUT TURNOVER . . .

Two countries have been through more than the usual number of regimes: Since gaining its independence from Spain in 1825, Bolivia has had nearly 200 different governments. And since the end of World War II in 1945, Italy has been through 57 governments.

CHUNNELING

The Eurostar Train connects the cities of Paris, London, and Brussels and creates a link—an underground channel tunnel popularly called the Chunnel—between Great Britain and continental Europe for the first time since they were geographically connected during the Ice Age. Traveling 23 miles at 150 feet under the English Channel, at a speed of about 100 miles per hour, the crossing now takes only about twenty minutes, and travelers can choose whether to ride as a passenger or bring their own cars on board.

The Chunnel, completed in 1994 after seven years of labor by 13,000 engineers and workers, was not a new idea. In 1802, French engineer Albert Mathieu-Favier put forth a proposal for a tunnel between England and France, in which passengers would ride in horse-drawn carriages. In 1875, both English and French parliaments passed bills for such a project—but the deadline passed before the necessary funds were raised. The $15 billion tunnel, one of Europe's largest infrastructure projects ever, was made financially possible by the Anglo-French TransManche Link, a consortium of ten construction companies and five banks from the two countries. Ironically, the Eurostar Train leaves from London's Waterloo Station—named for England's defeat of the French general Napoleon.

INTERROGATION TIME

The phrase "being given the third degree" most likely originated from the deep secrets of the Masonic organization. When a Freemason advances to the third level, or degree—referred to as master Mason—there is a careful examination of the person's background and qualifications.

THE LONG, LONG ROAD

The Appalachian Trail runs from Springer Mountain, Georgia, to Katahdin, Maine—a distance of 2,174 miles—and was the vision of forester Benton MacKaye. Since its inception in 1937, more than 8,000 people have reported hiking the entire trail. Many quit at the first town, about 20 miles up the trail; 15 percent quit in the first week, and only about 20 percent of hikers make it the whole way. The entire trip generally takes four to eight months.

The Canadians have added a 675-mile addition from Maine into Quebec called the International Appalachian Trail, though it is separate and not an official extension.

State	Miles of Trail
Maine	281.4
New Hampshire	161.0
Vermont	149.8
Massachusetts	90.2
Connecticut	51.6
New York	88.5
New Jersey	72.4
Pennsylvania	229.3
Maryland	40.8
West Virginia	4.0
Virginia	549.9
North Carolina	88.1
Tennessee	292.7
Georgia	75.2

◆

In PARAGUAY, dueling is still legal—as long as both parties are registered blood donors.

THE TOWN THAT BOOKS BUILT

There is a very small village in Wales in the Black Mountains near England called Hay-on-Wye. In the early 1960s a young man named Richard Booth opened a secondhand bookshop, eventually bought an old castle for the same purpose, and soon other entrepreneurs did the same. By 1988 the Annual Hay Festival began to showcase the wares of the town's booksellers, primarily antiquarian and used-book dealers. Today it is known worldwide as "The Town of Books," and it's no wonder: this little hamlet of 1,300 people currently boasts 39 bookshops.

◆

WORLD POLLUTION

Mexico City has the worst smog levels of any city on earth, followed by Beijing and Xian in China, and New Delhi, India. The U.S. cities most polluted by smog are:

1. Los Angeles (CA)
2. Visalia-Porterville (CA)
3. Bakersfield (CA)
4. Fresno (CA)
5. Houston (TX)
6. Merced (CA)
7. Sacramento (CA)
8. Hanford (CA)
9. Knoxville (TN)
10. Dallas–Fort Worth (TX)

◆

The CITY OF LOS ANGELES's full name is El Pueblo de Nuestra Senora la Reinade los Angeles de Porciuncula, which translates from the Spanish to "The Town of Our Lady the Queen of Angels of the Little Portion." ("Little Portion" referred to a small parcel of land.)

IT'S ALL ABOUT THE WHERE
A little bit of feng shui

Basic Tools
THINGS THAT WILL HELP FREE UP BLOCKAGES OF
ENERGY IN BOTH A HOME OR BUSINESS

Color: adds emotional, physiological, and
cultural content to life

Sound: connects us with others in our environment

Lighting, including fireplaces and garden lighting: brings
more life energy into the environment

Art: any kind that pleases you

Growing things: both plants and flowers

Water features: such as fountains, aquariums, and waterfalls

Wind-sensitive objects: wind chimes and other movement-
sensitive objects

Mirrors and crystals: circulate energy

THE BAGUAS, OR LIFE AREAS, AND THEIR
CORRESPONDING COLORS

Area	*Color*
Career	Black, Blue & Brown
Wisdom	Black, Blue & Green
Health & Family	Blue & Green
Wealth	Blue, Red & Purple
Reputation & Fame	Red

Area	Color
Love & Marriage	Red, Pink & White
Creativity & Children	White & Pastels
Helpful People	White, Gray & Black
Center or Chi	Yellow & Earth Tones

MEANING OF COLORS

Color	Meaning
Red	Attraction, Warmth, Strength
Green	Health, Potential
Purple	Spiritual guidance
Yellow	Energy, Life
Black	Mood, Perception
Pink	Love, Romance

AND A FEW FENG SHUI TIPS YOU SIMPLY MAY NOT BE ABLE TO FOLLOW:

Your apartment should not be on the top floor.

The main door should not be in front of the toilet.

Pictures showing cruelty or war scenes should not be hanging on the walls.

The dining room should have a fruit or vegetable picture on the wall.

Articles that cannot be repaired, especially watches, should not be kept in the house.

Oven burners should be kept clean.

BAD REPORT

The Committee to Protect Journalists is a nonprofit organization that promotes press freedom worldwide by defending the right of journalists to report the news without fear of reprisal. In their mission to publicly reveal journalistic abuses, the CPJ has released a list of its choices of the ten worst places in the world to be a journalist. These assignments are dangerous for a number of reasons, primarily lack of local journalistic freedoms, crackdowns from political regimes, and violent assaults on journalists:

West Bank	Burma
Columbia	Zimbabwe
Afghanistan	Iran
Eritrea	Kyrgyzstan
Belarus	Cuba

◆

SHOVELFESTS
Best North American Sandcastle Contests,
According to The Travel Channel

1. Myrtle Beach Open Sand Sculpting Competition, South Carolina (May)
2. World Championship Sand Sculpture, Harrison Hot Springs, British Columbia, Canada (September)
3. The Pizza Expo Sandtennial, Las Vegas, Nevada (April)
4. ExpoCité, Quebec, Canada (August)
5. Annual Port Aransas Sand Sculpture Contest, Texas (April)
6. U.S. Open Sandcastle Competition, Imperial Beach, California (July)
7. Annual Cannon Beach Sandcastle Contest, Oregon (June)

NOW BOARDING
Exactly where—and what—is Area 51?

Anything we suspect about Area 51 is just that: suspicion. Herewith, some of the more reliable ruminations on the tract of land we associate with aliens, UFOs, and secrecy.

- North of Las Vegas (at approximately longitude 115°45' and 115°56', and latitude 36°12.5' and 37°17.5') is a federally protected territory that covers an area equal to Rhode Island and Connecticut which is officially designated the Nellis Air Force Bombing and Gunnery Range.

- The draft version of the Environmental Impact Statement for the Nevada Test Site describes the origin of the block of land we know as Area 51: "Under Public Land Order 1662 (June 20, 1958), approximately 38,400 acres were reserved for the use of the Atomic Energy Commission in connection with the NTS. Management of this land has since been delegated to the U.S. Air Force." (Pages 4–9 to 4–11 of volume 1 of the EIS.)

- Area 51 is a tract of land six miles (north-south) by ten miles (east-west) bordered by the Nellis Bombing and Gunnery Range on the northwest, north, east, and south, and by the Nevada Test Site on the southwest. Area 51 is bounded, approximately, by longitude 115°45' and 115°56', and latitude and 36°12.5' and 37°17.5'.

- Reports are that more than 500 employees arrive at a guarded terminal at Las Vegas's McCarran Airport each day, where they board a small fleet of Boeing 737s that shuttle back and forth to Area 51.

IF YOU LIVED HERE

The most and least expensive cities from nearly 150 surveyed around the world

Most Expensive Cities

1. Tokyo, Japan
2. London, UK
3. Moscow, Russia
4. Osaka, Japan
5. Hong Kong
6. Geneva, Switzerland
7. Seoul, South Korea
8. Copenhagen, Denmark
9. Zürich, Switzerland
10. St. Petersburg, Russia

Least Expensive Cities

1. Asunción, Paraguay
2. Montevideo, Uruguay
3. Santo Domingo, Dominican Republic
4. Buenos Aires, Argentina
5. Harare, Zimbabwe
6. Bogotá, Colombia
7. Manila, Philippines
8. Bangalore, India
9. Quito, Ecuador
10. Blantyre, Malawi

◆

NORTH BY NORTH BY NORTH

Grid north is a navigational term referring to the direction northward along the grid lines of a map projection.

Magnetic north is the end of the planet where the earth's magnetic intensity is the greatest.

True north is a navigational term referring to the direction of the North Pole, relative to the navigator's position.

WATCH IT!

No matter how much time you think you're wasting in front of the television, chances are someone in the world has got you beat:

Location	TV Sets per Capita
1. Christmas Island	1,385.68 per 1,000 people
2. Bermuda	1,023.54 per 1,000 people
3. Monaco	778.08 per 1,000 people
4. United States	754.28 per 1,000 people
5. Malta	699.26 per 1,000 people
6. Japan	679.95 per 1,000 people
7. Canada	667.55 per 1,000 people
8. Norfolk Island	647.59 per 1,000 people
9. Guam	646.57 per 1,000 people
10. Luxembourg	627.53 per 1,000 people

Source: CIA World Factbook, December 2003

◆

THE MONEY MEN

The origin of the Medici family crest is also part of a familiar symbol seen around the world: a pawnbroker's sign. The Medicis, wealthy merchants and bankers in Florence from the fifteenth through the eighteenth centuries, were the largest moneylenders in Europe, and their crest is said to refer to a family story wherein a Medici fought a giant and killed him with a sack of three rocks. Those rocks became the three spheres in their emblem, and were subsequently immortalized as the trio of golden balls hanging outside the shops of moneylenders worldwide.

"THEY'RE HEEEERE"

An alien abduction is the forced removal of a person from his or her physical location to an unknown destination, presumably not on planet Earth. After the abduction, the person is returned to the original location and frequently has little or no recollection of the experience, and no idea where he or she might have been.

Common features of alien abductions include the feeling of paralysis; the perception of having been transported immaterially, frequently through a light beam; the sense of having been surgically probed or implanted with devices; the sense of freezing or slowing of time; and sexual or reproductive contact or manipulation by the aliens.

Alien and UFO believers cite indicators for those wondering whether or not they may be abductees. Some questions you might ask yourselves:

Have you lost time of any length, especially an hour or more?

Have you been paralyzed in bed with a being in your room?

Have you any unusual scars or marks with no explanation of how you received them (e.g., small scooplike indentations, scars in roof of mouth, nose, behind or in ears, genitals, etc.)?

Do you have a memory of flying through the air which you believe is not a dream?

Have you seen beams of light outside your home, or beams that enter your room through a window?

Have you had a strong sense of having a mission or an important task to perform, without knowing from where this compulsion comes?

Have you had a dream of eyes, such as animal eyes (like an owl's or deer's), or do you remember seeing an animal looking in at you from outside? Do you have a fear of eyes?

Do you have puzzling insomnia or sleep disorders?

Have you awoken in a place other than where you went to sleep—for example, in your car?

Have you seen someone become paralyzed, motionless, or frozen in time, especially someone you sleep with?

Have you known someone who claims to have witnessed a UFO or alien near you, or has said you have been missing?

Have you ever had the feeling of being watched, especially at night?

Have electronics around you gone haywire with no explanation, such as streetlights, televisions, and radios?

Do you believe that you have channeled telepathic messages from extraterrestrials?

Have you seen a hooded figure in or near your home, especially next to your bed?

According to the National UFO Reporting Center*, these are the places to keep your eyes on the skies:

Location	Reported Count
Unspecified/International	3,135
Alabama	236
Alaska	142
Alberta, Canada	167
Arizona	1,159

Location	Reported Count
Arkansas	313
British Columbia, Canada	553
California	3,950
Colorado	632
Connecticut	288
District of Columbia	46
Delaware	59
Florida	1,332
Georgia	439
Hawaii	121
Idaho	197
Illinois	1,007
Indiana	525
Iowa	247
Kansas	247
Kentucky	314
Louisiana	213
Maine	227
Manitoba, Canada	72
Maryland	305
Massachusetts	450
Michigan	766
Minnesota	394
Mississippi	166
Missouri	615
Montana	192
Nebraska	160
Nevada	426
New Brunswick, Canada	34
Newfoundland, Canada	11

Location	Reported Count
New Hampshire	176
New Jersey	536
New Mexico	326
New York	1,259
North Carolina	543
North Dakota	60
Northwest Territory	13
Nova Scotia, Canada	58
Ohio	928
Oklahoma	294
Ontario, Canada	662
Oregon	853
Pennsylvania	860
Prince Edward Island	8
Puerto Rico	36
Quebec, Canada	101
Rhode Island	87
Saskatchewan, Canada	39
South Carolina	252
South Dakota	66
Tennessee	455
Texas	1,456
Utah	285
Vermont	78
Virginia	454
Virgin Islands	2
Washington	2,088
West Virginia	179
Wisconsin	528
Wyoming	100

*As of June 2005

DIVE IN

The world's largest lake is actually the Caspian Sea, a salt-water lake measuring 143,200 square miles. It is surrounded by Russia, Azerbaijan, Iran, Turkmenistan, and Kazakhstan. The world's second-largest lake is also the world's largest freshwater lake: North America's Lake Superior, at 31,700 square miles.

Pirate stories and old salts often mention "The Seven Seas," which are actually the oceans of the worlds:

The Seven Seas
Northern Atlantic Ocean
Southern Atlantic Ocean
Northern Pacific Ocean
Southern Pacific Ocean
Indian Ocean
Southern Ocean
Arctic Ocean

◆

A PEACENIK IN THE OVAL OFFICE

The rumor has long been that the rug in the White House Oval Office changes depending on the state of the nation: that the eagle faces the arrows in his claw in times of war, and the olive branches in peacetime. There have been several rugs over the years, but in 1945 President Harry Truman had both the Presidential Seal and Flag redesigned for good. Truman felt that the eagle's head should never face the arrows of war. He believed that although the president should be prepared for war, he should always look toward peace, and had the head turned toward the olive branches.

ROUTE 66 REDUX

"The Mother Road." "The Main Street of America." "The Will Rogers Highway." These are all monikers for the road-tripper's paradise, Route 66. Today a traveler won't find a single original sign with that number—the last original Route 66 road sign was taken down in Chicago on January 17, 1977. The Mother Road (a term first used by John Steinbeck in *The Grapes of Wrath*) was decommissioned as a federal highway, with the last stretch disappearing from the records in 1984, replaced by interstates I-55, I-44, I-40, I-15, and I-10. Commissioned in 1926, this long and sometimes lonesome highway stretched for 2,448 miles across eight states (Illinois, Missouri, Kansas, Oklahoma, Texas, New Mexico, Arizona, and California) and three time zones, starting in Chicago and ending in Santa Monica; this was also the site of the eponymous TV series that ran from 1960 to 1964. When Route 66 was bypassed by superhighways in the 1960s, entire towns closed down, and businesses that had thousands of vehicles pass their way every day saw traffic dwindle to fewer than ten cars. About 85 percent of the original Route 66 can still actually be driven on. Today, Route 66 lives on in several books and Web sites.

WHERE TO LAY ONE'S WEARY HEAD

The most expensive hotel room in the world is the Imperial Suite at the President Wilson Hotel in Geneva, Switzerland. Four bedrooms, a study, a dressing room, a library, cocktail lounge, billiards, a dining room that seats 26, and bulletproof windows throughout add up to $33,000 a night. And yet you still have to check out at 11 A.M.

WHERE AM I?

Accident, Maryland
Aimwell, Alabama
America, Cambridgeshire, England
Arab, Alabama
Arabia, Finland
Arsenic Tubs, New Mexico
Atomic City, Idaho
Bat and Ball, Sevenoaks, Kent, England
Bat Cave, North Carolina
Beans Corner Bingo, Maine
Beer, Devon, England
Beer Bottle Crossing, Idaho
Big Arm, Montana
Big Ugly, West Virginia
Bird-in-Hand, Pennsylvania
Bitey Bitey, Pitcairn Island
Blow Me Down, Newfoundland, Canada
Bob, Canada
Bobo, Alabama
Bong Bong, New South Wales
Bottom, North Carolina
Bowlegs, Oklahoma
Bread Loaf, Vermont
Bucksnort, Tennessee
Bug, Kentucky
Bugscuffle, Tennessee
Bumble Bee, Arizona
Bumpass, Virginia
Bunlevel, North Carolina
Burnt Corn, Alabama

Cabbage Patch, California
Camel Hump, Wyoming
Carefree, Arizona
Cat Elbow Corner, New York
Chicken, Alaska
Chugwater, Wyoming
Clam, Virginia
Climax, Pennsylvania
Cold Christmas, Hertfordshire, England
Cool, California
Cuckoo, Virginia
Cut n' Shoot, Texas
Cut Off, Louisiana
Diagonal, Iowa
Difficult, Tennessee
Dildo Key, Florida
Dinosaur, Colorado
Disco, Tennessee
Dismal, Tennessee
Doghouse Junction, California
Do Stop, Kentucky
Double Trouble, New Jersey
Ecce Homo, Schwyz, Switzerland
Economy, Indiana
Eek, Alaska
Egg, Austria
Eighty Eight, Kentucky
Eighty Four, Pennsylvania
Elephant Butte, New Mexico
Eyebrow, Saskatchewan, Canada
Fear Not, Pennsylvania
Fertile, Minnesota
Flippin, Arkansas

Frankenstein, Missouri
Frostproof, Florida
Frying Pan, California
Gas, Kansas
Gay, Michigan
Grand Detour, Illinois
Gravity, Iowa
Hardup, Utah
Held For Certain, Kentucky
Hell, Michigan
Hellhole Palms, California
Hi Hat, Kentucky
HooHoo, West Virginia
Hot Coffee, Mississippi
How, Wisconsin
Humptulips, Washington
Hurt, Virginia
Hygiene, Colorado
Index, Washington
Intercourse, Pennsylvania
Jinks, Kentucky
Keg, California
Knockemstiff, Ohio
Last Chance, California
Latex, Louisiana
Left Hand, West Virginia
Lickskillet, Ohio
Little Penny, California
Lizard Lick, North Carolina
Looneyville, West Virginia
Lost Nation, New Hampshire
Loveladies, New Jersey
Manly, Iowa

Mars, Pennsylvania
Mary's Igloo, Alaska
Matching Tye, Essex, England
Meat Camp, North Carolina
Medicine Hat, Alberta, Canada
Metropolis, Illinois
Mexican Hat, Utah
Monkey's Eyebrow, Kentucky
Monster, Netherlands
Moose Factory, Ontario, Canada
Moose Jaw, Saskatchewan, Canada
Moron, Mongolia
Mosquitoville, Vermont
Mudsock, Ohio
Nasty, Hertfordshire, England
Needmore, Virginia
New Invention, West Midlands, England
Newtwopothouse, Ireland
Nightcaps, Southland, New Zealand
Nimrod, Minnesota
Ninety Six, South Carolina
No Guts Captain, Pitcairn Island
No Name Key, Florida
No Place, County Durham, England
Nothing, Arizona
Oblong, Illinois
Okay, Arkansas
Ordinary, Kentucky
Oven Fork, Kentucky
Paint Lick, Kentucky
Peculiar, Missouri
Peep-o-Day, near Wanganui, New Zealand
Pinch, West Virginia

Pity Me, County Durham, England
Police, Poland
Polkadotte, Ohio
Porcupine, South Dakota
Possum Grape, Arkansas
Pukë, Albania
Punkeydoodles Corners, Ontario, Canada
Purgatory, Maine
Pussy, Savoie, France
Puzzletown, Pennsylvania
Quick, West Virginia
Rabbit Hash, Kentucky
Rectum, The Netherlands
Rest and Be Thankful, Argyll and Bute, Scotland
River Styx, Ohio
Rottenegg, Upper Austria, Austria
Rough and Ready, California
Rum Jungle, Australia
Saddam Hussein, Sri Lanka
Saint-Louis-du-Ha! Ha!, Quebec, Canada
Sanatorium, Mississippi
Santa Claus, Georgia
Satan's Kingdom, Vermont
Secretary, Maryland
Secret Town, California
Seldom Seen Roadhouse, Victoria, Australia
Semen, Indonesia
Silly, Belgium
Skidoo, California
Sleepy Eye, Minnesota
Snafu Creek, Yukon, Canada
Snapfinger, Georgia
Soso, Mississippi

Spasticville, Kansas
Spit Junction, New South Wales, Australia
Splatt, Devon, England
Squabbletown, California
Sugar Tit, South Carolina
Surprise, Arizona
Swastika, Ontario, Canada
Sweet Lips, Tennessee
Thong, Kent, England
Tick Bite, North Carolina
Tincup, Colorado
Toadsuck, Perry County, Arkansas
Toast, North Carolina
Tombstone, Arizona
Twopothouse, Ireland
Useless Loop, Western Australia, Australia
Virgin, Utah
Wahoo, Nebraska
Wankers Corner, Oregon
Westward Ho!, Devon, England
Where Freddie Fall, Pitcairn Island
Where Minnie Off, Pitcairn Island
Where Reynolds Cut the Firewood, Pitcairn Island
Who'd Thought It, Texas
Why, Arizona
Whynot, North Carolina
Wide Open, Tyne and Wear, England
Wigtwizzle, South Yorkshire, England
Wink, Texas
Worms, Nebraska
You Bet, California
Zig Zag, Oregon
Zzyzx, California

SOME KIND OF HOT

A Land of Extremes: Death Valley days, nights, and other facts about one of the hottest, lowest, driest places on earth

TOTAL AREA: 3,372,402 acres

HIGHEST POINT:
Telescope Peak, 11,049 feet

LOWEST POINT:
Badwater: 282 feet below sea level, it is also the lowest point in the Western Hemisphere. During the Pleistocene era, the floor of Death Valley was the bottom of a vast lake.

HIGHEST TEMPERATURE:
134°F. In 2001, a new record was set when temperatures of over 100°F were recorded for 153 consecutive days.

LOWEST TEMPERATURE:
15°F, recorded January 8, 1913

ANNUAL RAINFALL:
1.96 inches

WATER SOURCES
Darwin Falls provides year-round water for plants and wildlife; Salt Creek, Travertine Springs, and other springs provide pockets of water in other parts of Death Valley.

ANIMALS & PLANTS:
Mammals: 51 species
Reptiles: 36 species
Amphibians: 5 species
Fish: 5 species
Birds: 346 species
Plants: 1,042 species

TAKING IT ON THE ROAD

The stops around the world where Bing Crosby and Bob Hope traveled in the "Road Pictures":

Road to Singapore (1940)
Road to Zanzibar (1941)
Road to Morocco (1942)
Road to Utopia (1946)
Road to Rio (1947)
Road to Bali (1952)
Road to Hong Kong (1962)

OH COME, ALL YE FAITHFUL

In 1995, the Supreme Court turned down an appeal by the Jennings Osborne family of Little Rock, Arkansas, who claimed that the state violated their religious beliefs when complaints from neighbors forced the Osbornes to drastically reduce the number of lights in their home's Christmas display. After losing the appeal, the Osbornes donated their collection, thought to be the largest in the world with three million lights, to Walt Disney World, where it has now grown to over five million lights, and has become the theme park's third-largest attraction. The Osbornes haven't lost that love-thy-neighbor feeling, though: They still sponsor light displays in 32 cities throughout Arkansas.

◆

The very FIRST BOMB dropped by the Allies on Berlin in World War II was just that—a bomb. The only thing it hit was an elephant in the Berlin Zoo.

FOLLOWING IN HIS FOOTSTEPS

In the early days after the crucifixion of Jesus Christ, people came to Jerusalem to see the holy sites connected with Jesus' death. Distance and the ravages of time eventually made it difficult for visits to continue for these pilgrims; consequently, the Stations of the Cross were developed in the Middle Ages as a Lenten devotion for Catholics around the world. It is a reenactment of the route in Jerusalem, the Via Dolorosa, that Jesus Christ followed to Calvary and his crucifixion. Traditionally, fourteen small shrines are set up in churches, and the supplicant follows the story of the Passion of the Christ—virtually in his footsteps.

The First Station:
Jesus Is Condemned to Die

The Second Station:
Jesus Carries His Cross

The Third Station:
Jesus Falls the First Time

The Fourth Station:
Jesus Meets His Mother

The Fifth Station:
Simon Helps Jesus Carry His Cross

The Sixth Station:
Veronica Wipes Jesus' Face

The Seventh Station:
Jesus Falls the Second Time

The Eighth Station:
Jesus Meets the Women of Jerusalem

The Ninth Station:
Jesus Falls the Third Time

The Tenth Station:
Jesus Is Stripped

The Eleventh Station:
Jesus Is Nailed to the Cross

The Twelfth Station:
Jesus Dies on the Cross

The Thirteenth Station:
Jesus Is Taken Down from the Cross

The Fourteenth Station:
Jesus Is Laid in the Tomb

◆

FANCY FOOTWORK

Tap dancing is a type of American theatrical dance, thought to be rooted as far back as the 1600s in the Irish jig and step dancing, English wooden shoe clog dancing, and African dance movements echoed and improvised upon by American slaves in the 1800s. Percussive footwork with precise rhythmic patterns is at the heart of tap dance, as its descriptive step names show—brush, flap, shuffle, ball change, cramp roll. By the 1920s the dancing became jazz-driven, and performers began to experiment with different types of metal plates, or taps, on their leather soles—and tap dancing became a true art form at last.

The word PANDEMONIUM, first used by John Milton in *Paradise Lost*, means the place of all demons. Other words for hell:

Abaddon
abyss
Apollyon
barathrum
blazes
everlasting fire
exterior darkness
furnace of fire
Gehenna
Hades
Hell
infernal region
inferno
netherworld
the pit
perdition
place of torments
pool of fire
Scheol
Tophet
underworld
unquenchable fire

The Five Rivers of Hell

Acheron—River of Woe
Cocytus—River of Lament
Lethe—River of Forgetfulness
Phlegethon—River of Fire
Styx—River of Oath

OLD IVY

The origin of the term Ivy League, though certainly referring to vine-covered college campuses, had nothing to do with the halls of education, and everything to do with their playing fields. Sportswriter Caswell Adams, from the *New York Herald-Tribune*, first used it in 1937 in reference to the conference of teams that was also known as the Old Ten: Army, Brown, Columbia, Cornell, Dartmouth, Harvard, Navy, Pennsylvania, Princeton, and Yale. In 1940, Navy and Army dropped out of the conference, but the rest had common athletic programs. The phrase soon began to cross over to represent the educational philosophies of the schools as well.

In 1927, a small group of women's colleges came together to promote the cause of all-women's education, and soon became known as the Seven Sisters:

Barnard

Bryn Mawr

Mount Holyoke

Radcliffe

Smith

Vassar

Wellesley

Vassar became coeducational in 1969, and Radcliffe has merged with Harvard; otherwise, the rest remain women's colleges.

◆

The Bronx, Brooklyn, Manhattan, Queens, and Staten Island were incorporated into one single entity—NEW YORK CITY—in 1898.

THE SMITHSONIAN MUSEUMS

The Smithsonian Institution, founded in 1826 by British scientist James Smithson, is the parent institution of the Smithsonian Museums, the largest museum complex in the world. The museums include:

- African Art Museum
- Air and Space Museum and the Steven F. Udvar-Hazy Center (Chantilly, Virginia)
- American Art Museum and its Renwick Gallery
- American History Museum
- American Indian Museum
- Anacostia Museum (African-American history and culture)
- Arts and Industries Building
- Cooper-Hewitt, National Design Museum (New York City)
- Freer and Sackler Galleries (Asian art)
- Hirshhorn Museum and Sculpture Garden (modern and contemporary art)
- National Museum of African-American History and Culture (in development)
- National Zoo
- Natural History Museum
- Portrait Gallery
- Postal Museum
- Smithsonian Institution Building, the Castle (visitor information)

All museums are in Washington, D.C., except where noted.

◆

RIKERS ISLAND, in New York City, is the largest penal colony in the world, with the population consistently around 13,000.

CRIMSON TIDE

On August 3, 1852, Yale and Harvard met for the nation's very first intercollegiate sporting event: a rowing contest at Lake Winnepesaukee, New Hampshire. The Cambridge crew prevailed over Yale by two lengths over a three-mile course. This set in motion a rivalry that thrives to this day. The Harvard and Yale crews now hold an annual four-mile race on the Thames River in New London, Connecticut, the longest of its kind in the country.

MURDER BY GEOGRAPHY

Countries throughout the world with the most intentional homicides per capita:

Rank	Country	Rate
1.	Colombia	0.62 per 1,000 people
2.	South Africa	0.51 per 1,000 people
3.	Jamaica	0.33 per 1,000 people
4.	Venezuela	0.33 per 1,000 people
5.	Russia	0.19 per 1,000 people
6.	Mexico	0.14 per 1,000 people
7.	Lithuania	0.10 per 1,000 people
8.	Estonia	0.10 per 1,000 people
9.	Latvia	0.10 per 1,000 people
10.	Belarus	0.10 per 1,000 people

◆

MONT BLANC, on the French-Italian border, is the highest mountain in the Alps at 15,771 feet.

OUR HOMES AWAY FROM HOME
Some of the world's best addresses—and all of them fictional

The Addams Family, 001 Cemetery Lane, USA

The Anderson family from *Father Knows Best*,
607 South Maple Street, USA

Batman (aka Bruce Wayne), Wayne Manor, Gotham City, USA

The Baxter family and their maid, Hazel,
123 Marshall Road, Hydsberg, NY

The Brady Bunch, 4222 Clinton Way, Los Angeles, California

The Bunker family from *All in the Family*,
704 Hauser Street, Queens, NY

Montgomery Burns, Homer's boss on *The Simpsons*,
1000 Mammon Street, Springfield, USA

Blake Carrington from *Dynasty*, 173 Essex Drive,
Denver, CO

The Clampett family from *The Beverly Hillbillies*, 518
Crestview Drive, Beverly Hills, CA

The Cleaver family from *Leave It to Beaver*, 485 Maple Drive
(later 211 Pine Street), Mayfield, USA

The Ewing family from *Dallas*, Southfork Ranch,
Braddock County, TX

Jessica Fletcher (aka J. P. Fletcher) from *Murder, She Wrote*, 698
Candlewood Lane, Cabot Cove, ME

Dr. Frasier Crane from *Frasier*, Apartment 1901, Elliot Bay
Towers, Seattle, WA

Sherlock Holmes, 221B Baker Street, London, UK

Ralph and Alice Kramden from *The Honeymooners*,
328 Chauncey Street, Brooklyn, NY

Leopold Bloom from the James Joyce novel *Ulysses*,
7 Eccles Street, Dublin, Ireland

Agent Fox Mulder from *The X-Files*, 42-2630 Hegal Place,
Alexandria, VA

The Munsters, 1313 Mockingbird Lane,
Mockingbird Heights, USA

Oscar Madison and Felix Unger from *The Odd Couple*,
1049 Park Avenue, New York, NY

The Partridge Family, 698 Sycamore Road,
San Pueblo, CA

The Petrie family from *The Dick Van Dyke Show*, 448 Bonnie
Meadow Road, New Rochelle, NY

The Ricardo family from *I Love Lucy*, Apartment 4A (later
3D), 623 East 68th Street, New York, NY

Mary Richards from *The Mary Tyler Moore Show*, Apartment D,
119 North Weatherly Avenue, Minneapolis, MN

Jerry Seinfeld, Apartment 5A, 129 West 81st Street,
New York, NY

The Simpsons, 742 Evergreen Terrace, Springfield, USA

The Stephens family from *Bewitched*,
1164 Morning Glory Circle, Westport, CT

Buffy Summers from *Buffy the Vampire Slayer*,
1630 Revello Drive, Sunnydale, CA

WHEEE!

The oldest amusement park in the world is in Bakken, Denmark, dating back to 1583. It was one of the premier "pleasure gardens" of medieval Europe, the forerunner of what we think of today as the amusement park, featuring entertainment, fireworks, games, and even primitive rides. Originally these sites were often a town's public garden, and ball games and shooting galleries started springing up, commercializing them. They continued to be popular into eighteenth-century Europe, when political unrest brought the end to such frivolity. By the late 1800s, the growth in interest in these parks switched from Europe to the United States, with a little help from newly formed trolley companies that were looking for ways to encourage ridership. The parks offered picnic facilities, dance halls, restaurants, games, and a few amusement rides—often on the shores of a lake or river, and at the end of the trolley line.

The Chicago World's Fair brought the modern amusement park into its golden age, with the introduction of both the Ferris wheel and the midway, a long stretch of food and game concessions and rides.

Soon the parks were known more for the excitement of their rides rather than their pastoral locations, and in 1895 the twain met in the development of perhaps the world's most famous amusement park of all: Coney Island. Then, in 1955, "The Happiest Place on Earth" opened: Walt Disney produced his dream park at Disneyland, taking the genre a step further by developing the theme park, eschewing typical rides for the fantasy of different "worlds" for guests to visit. Ironically, the success of the theme park has spread across the Atlantic and around the world, bringing the "pleasure gardens" back home again.

PARADISES FOUND
A selection of beaches most often mentioned as the best in the world

Anse Source d'Argent, La Digue, Seychelles
Cancun, Mexico
Clifton Beach, Cape Town, South Africa
Copacabana, Brazil
Crete, Greece
Datai Beach, Langkawi, Malaysia
Fraser Island, Australia
Grand Cul-de-Sac, St. Bart's
Ipanema, Rio de Janeiro, Brazil
Kuta Bali, Indonesia
Larvotto Beach, Monte Carlo, Monaco
The Maldives Islands
Maroma Beach, Mexico
Mauna Kea, Hawaii
Natadola Beach, Fiji
Negril, Jamaica
Paradise Beach, Mykonos Island, Greece
Paradise Island, Bahamas
Patong Beach, Phuket Island, Thailand
Phi Phi Island, Langkawi, Thailand
Pink Sands, Bahamas
Poipu Beach, Kauai, Hawaii
South Beach, Florida
Surfers Paradise, Australia
Tenerife, Canary Islands
Waikiki, Hawaii

◆

Every continent has a city named ROME.

LEFT-HANDERS

Places around the world where you must drive on the left

Anguilla
Antigua and Barbuda
Australia
Bangladesh
Barbados
Bhutan
Brunei
Bahamas
Bermuda
Botswana
Caymen Islands
Christmas Island (Australia)
Cook Islands
Cyprus
Dominica
East Timor
Falkland Islands
Fiji
Grenada
Guernsey (Channel Islands)
Guyana
Hong Kong
India
Indonesia
Ireland
Isle of Man
Jamaica
Japan
Jersey (Channel Islands)
Kenya

Kiribati
Kneeling (Cocos) Islands (Australia)
Lesotho
Macau
Malta
Malawi
Malaysia
Maldives
Mauritania
Montserrat
Mozambique
Namibia
Nauru
Nepal
New Zealand
Niue
Norfolk Island (Australia)
Pakistan
Papua New Guinea
Pitcairn Islands (Britain)
Saint Helena
Saint Kitts and Nevis
Seychelles
Singapore
Solomon Islands
South Africa
Sri Lanka
St. Lucia
St. Vincent and Grenadines

Suriname
Swaziland
Tanzania
Thailand
Tokelau (New Zealand)
Tonga
Trinidad and Tobago
Turks and Caicos

Tuvalu
Uganda
United Kingdom
Virgin Islands (U.S. and
British)
Zambia
Zimbabwe

◆

BRIDGES OVER SEVERAL WATERS
Where to see some of the most fascinating connectors in the world

- The very short Baily Bridge, 98 feet long, is the highest
  bridge in the world at 18,379 feet above sea level. Built by
  the Indian Army in 1982, it spans the Ladakh Valley,
  between the Dras and Suru Rivers, in the Himalayas.
- The longest bridge in the world that is built completely
  over water is the Pontchartrain Causeway in New Orleans,
  constructed in 1956 with a total length of 24 miles.
- The world's largest natural bridge is also a natural wonder:
  the Rainbow Bridge, at the base of Navajo Mountain, at the
  edge of Lake Powell in Utah. It reaches 290 feet from its
  base to the top of the arch, and spans 275 feet across the
  Colorado River. The top of the arch is 42 feet thick and 33
  feet wide.

NOT IN THE USSR
The USSR broke into fifteen new countries in 1991:

Armenia * Azerbaijan * Belarus * Estonia * Georgia
* Kazakhstan * Kyrgyzstan * Latvia * Lithuania * Moldova
* Russia * Tajikistan * Turkmenistan * Ukraine * Uzbekistan

ABC'S AROUND THE WORLD
Where children stay in school the longest

Rank	Country	Years Educated
1.	Norway	16.9
2.	Finland	16.7
3.	Australia	16.6
4.	United Kingdom	16.4
5.	New Zealand	16.2
6.	Sweden	16.0
7.	Netherlands	15.9
8.	Belgium	15.8
9.	Iceland	15.8
10.	Denmark	15.6
11.	France	15.4
12.	Germany	15.3
13.	Spain	15.3
14.	United States	15.2
15.	Portugal	15.2
16.	Switzerland	15.0
17.	Ireland	14.9
18.	Canada	14.8
19.	Austria	14.7
20.	Italy	14.7

Source: UNESCO Institute for Statistics

◆

The most SENSITIVE parts of the body have the most touch receptors—like the lips, tongue, fingertips, and soles of the feet. One of the least sensitive areas of the body is the middle of the back.

WHERE AM I?

A maze is predominantly a horticultural puzzle commonly
found in landscape gardening and based on the Greek labyrinth
in Crete—the home of the minotaur killed by Theseus, who
found his way out of the labyrinth by following a string. Over
time, a maze has taken on a different connotation than a
labyrinth; the former is designed to be a puzzle, while the latter
is an unambiguous through-route and is not designed to be
difficult to navigate. Built with complex branching passages
often made of high hedges, a maze is designed so that both the
center and the exit are difficult for the walker, or solver, to find.
A prominent feature of the formal English gardens of the
seventeenth and eighteenth centuries—most notably Hampton
Court Palace, London—mazes are presently enjoying a
renaissance as a meditative and spiritual tool.

Mathematician Leonhard Euler was one of the first to
analyze mazes, and in doing so founded the science of topology.
The best rule for traversing mazes is the Wall Follower, also
known as either the "left-hand rule" or the "right-hand rule."
By consistently keeping a hand in contact with the maze's wall,
one is guaranteed not to get lost, and either reach the exit, if
there is one, or return to the entrance. Other options, including
the Pledge Algorithm (which utilizes a compass) or Tremaux's
Algorithm (a version of Theseus's escape plan), are more
complex methods of escape. The last rule, called Random
Mouse, is nearly self-explanatory: If at first you don't succeed…

SPELL IT OUT

The "ABC Islands" is the nickname given to the Caribbean
resort spots of Aruba, Bonaire, and Curacao.

WORLD RELIGIOUS SITES
Some holy destinations, shrines, and pilgrimages

Amritsar, India: site of the Golden Temple of the Sikhs

Axum, Ethiopia: Ethiopian Orthodox believe the Ark of the
Covenant is kept here

Bethlehem, Israel: birthplace of Jesus Christ

Black Hills, South Dakota: Lakota Indians' site
for sacred vision quests

Bodhi Gaya, India: where Buddha reached enlightenment

Canterbury, England: seat of the Anglican archbishop

Dharamsala, India: seat of the Dalai Lama in exile

Fatima, Portugal: Catholics believe this to be the site of
1917 visions of the Virgin Mary

Ganges River, India: Hindus immerse themselves
here for spiritual purification

Haifa, Israel: seat of the Baha'i faith

Istanbul, Turkey: Eastern Orthodox seat of the
patriarchate of Constantinople

Jerusalem, Israel: world's only holy site for Judaism,
Christianity, and Islam

Kusinagar, India: site of the Buddha's death

Lhasa (Zhangmu), Tibet: sacred site for Tibetan Buddhists of
Potala Palace, historical abode of the Dalai Lama

Lourdes, France: Catholics believe springs have been curative
here since St. Bernadette's visions in 1858

Lumbini, Nepal: birthplace of Buddha

Mecca, Saudi Arabia: the center of Islam, birthplace of
Muhammad, and destination of the *hajj*, the Muslim
pilgrimage

Medina, Saudi Arabia: the Muslim holy city, home of
Muhammad after his escape from Mecca in 622 C.E.

Palitana, India: Shatrunjaya Hill, home to 863 temples,
is the pilgrimage destination for Jains

Salt Lake City, Utah: seat of the Church of Jesus
Christ of Latter-Day Saints

The Vatican: seat of Catholicism and home to the pope

ANOTHER RAINY DAY IN PARADISE

The Tumucumaque Mountains National Park in Brazil is the
world's largest rain forest state park, covering 9,562,770 acres
of remote, unexplored forests in Amapá. Bordered by the
northern Amazon River and French Guyana, the park is larger
than Massachusetts and Connecticut combined. At least eight
primate species, 350 bird species and 37 lizard species live in
these forests. Several other species represent endangered
populations, including the jaguar, giant anteater, giant
armadillo, harpy eagle, the black spider monkey, the brown-
bearded saki monkey, and the white-faced saki monkey.

The oldest working LIGHTHOUSE in the world is at La
Coruña in northwestern Spain, near the town of Ferol. A
lighthouse has been on this site since the time of the Roman
emperor Trajan (98–117 C.E.). The current lighthouse was
renovated and altered in 1682 and again in 1778.

ACTION!

Labor law describes a movie studio as any location where movies are made and also the company that produces, promotes, and distributes them. If this is so, the ramshackle tar structure Thomas Edison built in West Orange, New Jersey, in 1892 fits the bill. It cost $637.67, the roof opened so the sun could shine on the twelve-foot stage, and they called it the "Black Maria." Within a few years, companies began to move west to California—not only for the good weather, but because Edison's Motion Picture Patents Company couldn't keep an eye on their work as easily out west. The inventor owned almost every patent relevant to movie production at the time.

Nestor Studios opened in 1911 in the area soon to be called Hollywood, and as soon as the talkies took over, the mergers began (and haven't stopped since). Five large companies, Fox (later 20th Century Fox), Loew's Incorporated (later Metro-Goldwyn-Mayer), Paramount Pictures, Warner Bros., and RKO (Radio-Keith-Orpheum), began functioning as producers, promoters, distributors, and exhibitors, and the studio system took off.

◆

I, ROBOT

Robots were a literary conceit before they were real. Webster defines robot as "an automatic device that performs functions normally ascribed to humans, or a machine in the form of a human." In 1921, acclaimed Czech playwright Karel Capek (1890–1938) introduced the word in *R.U.R.* (Rossum's Universal Robots). *Robot* was a Czech word for forced laborer or serf; Capek's play presents robots initially as a boon to people, but they become the cause of unemployment and social unrest.

EAGLES, BIRDIES, AND JASMINE

Each hole of the famed Augusta National Golf Club, home of the renowned Masters tournament, is named after flora found on the course. Here's where to catch a "birdie's eye view."

1st	Tea Olive
2nd	Pink Dogwood
3rd	Flowering Peach
4th	Flowering Crabapple
5th	Magnolia
6th	Juniper
7th	Pampas
8th	Yellow Jasmine
9th	Carolina Cherry
10th	Camellia
11th	White Dogwood
12th	Golden Bell
13th	Azalea
14th	Chinese Fir
15th	Firethorn
16th	Redbud
17th	Nandina
18th	Holly

◆

WHERE DID YOU HEAR THAT?

Though foul words, dialects, and vernacular are likely as old as language itself, the first volume that recorded "English slang" was Captain Francis Grose's *A Classical Dictionary of the Vulgar Tongue*. It was first published in 1785; today the U.S. Library of Congress lists 169 slang dictionaries.

BLAST OFF!
Troposphere, stratosphere, mesosphere—and you're out of here!

Outer space is out there all right—but where? The atmosphere thins with increasing altitude, even on terra firma, but the actual place where atmosphere turns into space is vague. The Fédération Aéronautique Internationale uses 62 miles (100 km)—known as the Karman Line—as the boundary between atmosphere and space, but there are other steps along the way:

1.86 miles (3 km)	U.S. Federal Aviation Administration requires supplemental oxygen for aircraft pilots and passengers
9.94 miles (16 km)	pressurized cabin or pressure suit required
11.18 miles (18 km)	troposphere ends
14.91 miles (24 km)	aircraft pressurization systems no longer function
19.88 miles (32 km)	turbojets no longer function
27.96 miles (45 km)	ramjets no longer function
31.07 miles (50 km)	stratosphere ends
49.71 miles (80 km)	mesosphere ends
62.14 miles (100 km)	aerodynamic surfaces no longer function
75.81 miles (122 km)	reentry from orbit begins

In the United States, persons who travel above an altitude of 50 miles (80 km) are designated as astronauts.

◆

Siberia's LAKE BAIKAL is the only lake in the world that is deep enough to have deep-sea fish.

THE MYSTERY OF THE GIRL SCOUT COOKIE

Like Santa Claus, they come once a year. A strange and unique variety of cookies, hand-sold by Girl Scouts. Where *do* they come from? Currently only two licensed bakers supply local Girl Scout councils:

ABC/Interbake Foods (40 percent of cookies) bill themselves in their company literature as "the oldest and most experienced licensed Girl Scout Cookie baker. We became 'Official Girl Scout Cookie Bakers' in 1939, just two years after the first sale of commercially baked Girl Scout cookies took place. ABC is part of Interbake Foods LLC, a Richmond, Virginia–based manufacturer that has been baking cookies and crackers for 100 years." ABC makes Thin Mints, Peanut Butter Sandwiches, Shortbread, Caramel deLites, Peanut Butter Patties, Reduced Fat Lemon Pastry Cremes, Animal Treasures, and Iced Berry Piñatas for the Girl Scouts.

Little Brownie Bakers (60 percent of cookies) have been baking Girl Scout cookies for over twenty-five years and provide eight varieties of cookies for the annual Cookie Sale, including Samoas, Thin Mints, Tagalongs, Do-si-dos, Trefoils, and All Abouts.

REPTILIAN MALARKEY

It's a nice legend, but full of blarney: St. Patrick didn't drive the snakes out of Ireland—ice did. No snakes survived the glaciers that covered the Isle of Erin after the last Ice Age, about 15,000 years ago. The island is isolated far enough away across the Irish Sea from England that the snakes have never been able to return. Or maybe St. Patrick just asked politely . . .

HIGH-LOW: THE TOP AND BOTTOM OF THE WORLD

Mount Everest

It's approximately 5.5 miles high, and though the exact height is disputed, current readings count Everest at 29,035 feet.

Dead Sea

Bordering Jordan and Israel, it is the lowest point on earth that is on land, at 1,312 feet below sea level.

Marianas Trench

The lowest underwater point on earth is in the Pacific Ocean near Guam—it is 36,201 feet deep.

EARLY AMERICAN VITICULTURE

"The birthplace of American viticulture" isn't Sonoma or Napa, or even Long Island's North Shore. It's a spot in New York's Hudson River Valley—a planting in 1827 at Croton Point, to be exact—where the nation's oldest continually operating vineyard started. Wine was made from grapes from this region by the French Huguenots in the seventeenth century (Huguenots also helped early Americans in St. Augustine, Florida, grow the hearty muscadine in the late sixteenth century). In the early 1800s, Andrew Jackson Caywood bought and planted a piece of land that had been growing grapes since 1772; it was later incorporated as the Village of Marlborough. Cayman created hearty hybrids that anticipated some French varieties by nearly a dozen years. In 1957, the property was sold and renamed Benmarl—and the new owners carry on Caywood's legacy of experimental winemaking.

ALL OVER YOUR BODY
Odd places you may not know you even have

Glabella: The space between the eyebrows, just above the nose.

Uvula: The pendent fleshy lobe in the middle of the posterior border of the soft palate.

Canthus: The corner where the upper and under eyelids meet on each side of the eye.

Axilla: The armpit, or the cavity beneath the junction of the arm and shoulder.

Frenum: A connecting fold of membrane serving to support or restrain any part, as of the tongue.

Lunula: The crescent-shaped area at the base of the human fingernail.

A SEA THAT IS AT SEA

The Sargasso Sea is the only body of water in the world without a shoreline; it's completely surrounded by the North Atlantic. Oval-shaped and filled with vast amounts of seaweed, it encompasses thousands of square miles and slowly rotates clockwise. It's considered a sea because it is essentially a body of water completely different than the Atlantic in which it lies: It has its own unique ecosystem, with organisms that are specially adapted to live among the unusual Sargassum seaweed, and has currents that move at a different rate than those around it—giving it an all-water "shoreline" of its own. It appears as a floating lens of warm, exceptionally clear water, and it drifts, its location determined by the changing ocean currents.

THE VAGUE HAGUE
The Hague: What exactly is *it? A few facts* . . .

The Hague is the administrative capital and the third-largest city in the Netherlands after Amsterdam, its capital, and Rotterdam. Amsterdam is the nominal national capital; the Dutch government, the seat of the Crown (Queen Beatrix), and the supreme court are located in The Hague.

The Hague is located in the western part of the country, in the province South Holland, of which it is also the capital.

Founded in 1248 by William II, Count of Holland and King of Germany, The Hague had a population of nearly 475,000 in 2004.

The Hague Conventions of 1899 and 1907 were, along with the Geneva Conventions, among the first formal statements of the laws of war and war crimes in the body of international law.

The United Nations names The Hague as one of its capitals; thus it is host to several institutions of the UN:

The International Court of Justice, located in the Peace Palace, Vredespaleis (its construction was financed by Andrew Carnegie)

The International Criminal Tribunal for the Former Yugoslavia

The International Criminal Court

The Organization for the Prohibition of Chemical Weapons

The Model United Nations

Other famous institutions in The Hague are:

Permanent Court of Arbitration

Organization for Prohibition of Chemical Weapons (OPCW)

European Patent Office

Europol

In the near future the city will also welcome the Organization for Prohibition of Biological Weapons.

◆

YO! HO! HO! AND NO BOTTLE OF RUM

A major change in U.S. naval regulations came down with the appointment of Secretary of the Navy Josephus Daniels in 1913. He prohibited alcohol aboard all naval vessels—making strong coffee the strongest quaff around. In a mock salute, sailors began to call it "a cup of Joe." Current regulations state that if a ship is at sea for forty-five consecutive days the captain can authorize a special ration of two cans of beer per crew member. Otherwise, navy ships still remain dry.

GROUND ROUTE
Freedom in a box

Henry "Box" Brown was born a slave in Louisa County, Virginia, in 1815. He married and had children, but when his family was sold to a plantation owner in North Carolina in 1849, he decided to escape, and procured the help of a southern shoemaker. The sympathetic friend arranged for him to be shipped to Philadelphia in a box. Brown not only survived, but became a renowned anti-slavery speaker and wrote his autobiography, *Narrative of the Life of Henry Box Brown*.

R. I. P.

Final resting places of the famous, infamous, or unknown, and some of the world's renowned burial sites

Basilica di Santa Croce di Firenze, Florence, Italy: Galileo, Machiavelli, Michelangelo, Gioacchino Rossini, and many other notables are laid to rest here, perhaps opened by St. Francis himself in 1294.

Cimetière du Père Lachaise, Paris, France: Founded in 1805, this famous resting place is the final home to many French Holocaust victims; also the resting place of Oscar Wilde, Jim Morrison, and Frederic Chopin.

Cimitero Monumentale, Milan, Italy: On the grounds of this vast cemetery founded in 1860 is the *Famedio,* or Temple of Fame, where Giuseppe Verdi, Vladimir Horowitz, Alessandro Manzoni, and Arturo Toscanini are interred.

Fairview Cemetery, Fairfax, Nova Scotia: Though founded in 1832, this cemetery made history in 1912 when it became the Titanic Cemetery, where 121 victims of the maritime disaster were laid to rest. Each grave says the same thing: Besides the victim's name, it reads only "Died April 15, 1912."

The Great Pyramid of Giza: This is the last of the Seven Wonders of the World (allegedly 2570 B.C.E.), and probably the most renowned cemetery in the world. It presumably serves as the tomb of the Fourth Dynasty Egyptian Pharaoh Cheops.

Catholic Cemetery, Mount Zion, Jerusalem, Israel: In almost continual use from the time of the First Temple (ca. 850 to 586 B.C.E.) until the present. Oskar Schindler is buried here.

Novodevichy Cemetery, Moscow, Russia: Many famous Russians and citizens of the former Soviet Union have been buried here since its founding in 1524, including Nikita Khrushchev, Anton Chekhov, and composers Sergei Prokofiev and Dmitri Shostakovich.

Peter and Paul Fortress, St. Petersburg, Russia: All Russian czars since Peter the Great are buried in the cathedral, built between 1703 and 1728.

Rockwood Cemetery, Sydney, Australia: The largest burial site in the Southern Hemisphere, founded in 1867, is the final resting place of approximately one million souls.

Westminster Abbey, London, England: Eighteen monarchs and England's most notable statesmen and distinguished subjects have been laid to rest in the Abbey since Henry III began its rebuilding in 1245. Since the fourteenth century, the Abbey has become a burial place for notables such as Charles Darwin, Sir Isaac Newton, Robert Browning, Geoffrey Chaucer, Charles Dickens, George Frederick Handel, Thomas Hardy, Rudyard Kipling, Laurence Olivier, and Alfred, Lord Tennyson.

◆

AN EVERYMAN FOR EVERYWHERE

On June 20, 1970, David Kunst set out from Waseca, Minnesota, to walk 14,450 miles around the world. He made it—four years, three months, sixteen days, and 21 pairs of shoes later. It is to date the only certified walk around the world (he flew across the oceans) and is listed in *The Guinness Book of World Records*.

THINKING GLOBALLY

The Greeks are considered to be the founders of geography as a scientific discipline. In 140 B.C.E., a Greek named Crates is said to have created the first globe, a spherical representation of Earth; today the globe is still considered to be the most spatially accurate depiction of Earth.

The world's largest globe is the Unisphere, built for the 1964 New York World's Fair at Flushing Meadows, New York. This stainless steel globe is 120 feet across and weighs 900,000 pounds. The three rings around it trace the orbits of Yuri Gagarin, the first man in space; John Glenn, the first American to orbit Earth; and Telstar, the first communications satellite. Its motto: "Peace Through Understanding."

LOST WEEK-AND-A-HALF

On September 2, 1752, time flew like never before in both England and its American colonies, when the Gregorian calendar replaced the Julian calendar. On the day calendars changed, the world was suddenly eleven days ahead of where it had been. People went to bed on September 2 . . . and woke up on September 14.

PENNSYLVANIA CRUDE

The first successful oil well in the world gushed on an August day in 1859, and in a rather surprising spot: Titusville, in northwestern Pennsylvania. Colonel Edwin L. Drake was certain that extracting oil from the earth by drilling was the way of the future, and set aside enough money to drill 1,000 feet. He struck black gold at 69½ feet.

HANGAR STAKES

Everett, Washington, is home to the Boeing Aircraft Plant, a major aircraft manufacturing location that offers visitors factory tours that showcase Boeing and invites visitors to enter what the company claims is the largest building in the world: 472 million cubic feet of space, almost 100 acres. Guests—and there are 120,000 of them a year—see airplanes in various stages of flight tests and how the company tailors its aircraft for different countries and carriers around the world.

◆

BUT THEY'RE NOT MADE OF HAM

"Hamburgers, hamburgers, hamburgers hot; onions in the middle, pickle on top. Makes your lips go flippity flop."

There are several claims to the origin of the hamburger in the United States, from Charlie Nagreen of Seymour, Wisconsin, who composed the haunting melody above for the 1885 Outagamie County Fair, to the traveling Menches Brothers from Akron, Ohio, who claim they invented the patty sandwich in the same year. There is even a mention of a "hamburg steak" on the 1827 menu of Delmonico's in New York, though exactly what it was remains unknown. But the earliest references seem to come from the days of Genghis Khan, when his army would carry pieces of lamb or beef under their saddles to soften the meat, then grind it and eat it one-handed while riding horseback. When Ghengis's grandson, Kublai Khan, invaded Moscow in 1238, the Russians began to make their own changes to the recipe, adding chopped onion, raw eggs, and spices and naming it after the invaders: Steak Tartare.

SAIL AWAY
The inhabited islands of the Caribbean

Anguilla (UK)

Antigua and Barbuda
Antigua
Barbuda

Aruba (Netherlands)

Barbados
Barbados
Culpepper Island
Pelican Island (now
absorbed into Barbados)

Belize
Ambergris Caye
Caye Caulker
Glover's Reef
Lighthouse Reef
South Water Caye
Turneffe Islands

British Virgin Islands (UK)
Anegada
Beef Island
Bellamy Cay
Cooper Island
Frenchman's Cay
Great Camanoe
Guana Island
Jost Van Dyke
Little Thatch
Marina Cay

Mosquito Island
Nanny Cay
Necker Island
Norman Island
Peter Island
Prickly Pear Island
Saba Rock
Salt Cay
Tortola
Virgin Gorda

Cayman Islands (UK)
Cayman Brac
Grand Cayman
Little Cayman

Colombia
San Andrés and Providencia

Cuba
Cuba
Isla de la Juventud

Dominica

Grenada
Carriacou
Grenada
Petit Martinique

Guadeloupe (France)
Basse-Terre
La Désirade

Grande-Terre
Marie-Galante
Iles de la Petite-Terre
Saint-Barthélemy
Terre-de-Bas (Les Saintes)
Terre-de-Haut (Les Saintes)
Saint-Martin (same island as Sint Maarten)

Hispaniola (Haiti and the Dominican Republic)

Honduras
Barbaretta (Islas de la Bahía Department)
Cayos Cochinos (Islas de la Bahía)
Guanaja (Islas de la Bahía)
Roatán (Islas de la Bahía)
Swan Islands
Útila (Islas de la Bahía)

Jamaica

Martinique (France)

Mexico
Cancún
Isla Contoy
Isla Cozumel
Isla Mujeres

Montserrat (UK)

Netherlands Antilles (Netherlands)
Bonaire

Curaçao
Saba
Sint Eustatius
Sint Maarten (same island as Saint-Martin)

Nicaragua
Corn Islands
Cayos Miskitos

Panama
San Blas Islands
Bocas del Toro

Puerto Rico (U.S.)
Culebra
Mona
Puerto Rico
Vieques

Saint Kitts and Nevis
Nevis
Saint Kitts

Saint Lucia

Saint Vincent and the Grenadines
Bequia
Canouan
Mayreau
Mustique
Palm Island
Petit Saint Vincent
Saint Vincent
Union Island
Young Island

Trinidad and Tobago
Tobago
Trinidad

Turks and Caicos (UK)
Grand Turk
Middle Caicos
North Caicos
Parrot Cay
Pine Cay
Providenciales
Salt Cay

South Caicos

U.S. Virgin Islands
Hassel Island
Saint Croix
Saint John
Saint Thomas
Water Islan

Venezuela
Isla Margarita
Los Roques
Los Testigos

NO MAN'S LAND?

In 1861, the British government defined "island": If it was inhabited, then the size of the piece of land was of no import. If no one lived on the land, it had to be the size of "the summer's pasturage of at least one sheep"—which is about two acres.

Bishop Rock is commonly considered the smallest island in the world. Off the Scilly Islands in Cornwall, UK, it has only a lighthouse and takes perhaps the worst buffeting by the ocean on earth (the first tower, erected in 1847, was swept away before it was even operable).

"Where all the women are strong, all the men are good-looking, and all the chidren are above average."

—GARRISON KEILLOR'S DESCRIPTION OF THE FICTIONAL
LAKE WOEBEGON, MINNESOTA, ON RADIO'S
Prairie Home Companion

KITTY HEAVEN

In Key West, Florida, the streets are filled not only with loose chickens and roosters, but countless six-toed cats. Many of them are believed to be descendants of a feline given to the writer Ernest Hemingway. Local legend has it he was penning *The Old Man and the Sea* at the time, and a drinking buddy, who was also a sea captain, gave him a polydactyl cat. Sea lore has it that six-toed cats are good luck for sailors (and are superior mousers). Hemingway brought the kitty home, and his Key West house, which is now a museum, cares for more than sixty "Hemingway cats" to this very day. Most of the family are six-toed, and many of them are named after other writers or movie stars. Presently on location are Somerset Maugham, Emily Dickinson, Archibald MacLeish, Simone de Beauvoir, Zelda Fitzgerald, Trevor Howard, Marilyn Monroe, Joan Crawford, Charlie Chaplin, and Ava Gardner—to name just a few.

THIS OLD HOUSE

Outside of Tokyo, Japanese archaeologists have recently discovered ten post holes forming two irregular pentagons: They are mostly likely the remains of two huts, and what seem to be the world's oldest artificial structures. Thought to be built by *Homo erectus*, who were known to use simple tools, the site is about 500,000 years old.

REYKJAVIK, ICELAND, is the world's northernmost capital, with a population of approximately 180,000 people. The city was settled in the year 874.

THE RICHEST OF THE RICH

A country's wealth is defined by its gross domestic product (GDP), or value of all final goods and services produced within that nation in a given year. These estimates are derived from purchasing power parity calculations.

Country	Amount
1. Luxembourg	$58,900 per person
2. United States	$40,100 per person
3. Guernsey	$40,000 per person
4. Norway	$40,000 per person
5. Jersey	$40,000 per person
6. British Virgin Islands	$38,500 per person
7. Bermuda	$36,000 per person
8. San Marino	$34,600 per person
9. Hong Kong	$34,200 per person
10. Switzerland	$33,800 per person
11. Cayman Islands	$32,300 per person
12. Denmark	$32,200 per person
13. Ireland	$31,900 per person
14. Iceland	$31,900 per person
15. Canada	$31,500 per person
16. Austria	$31,300 per person
17. Australia	$30,700 per person
18. Belgium	$30,600 per person
19. United Kingdom	$29,600 per person
20. Netherlands	$29,500 per person
21. Japan	$29,400 per person
22. Finland	$29,000 per person
23. France	$28,700 per person
24. Germany	$28,700 per person
25. Isle of Man	$28,500 per person

Source: CIA World Factbook 2005

NO SMALL MALL

It's not "the mall" most of us think of when we hop in the car to hit the movies and run a few errands. The West Edmonton Mall, in Alberta, Canada, is not only the world's largest mall, but also bills itself as the world's largest shopping, amusement, and recreation center, attracting millions of tourists every year; the mall's economic impact on the Province of Alberta surpasses that of even Banff National Park. It employs over 23,000 people, covers over 5.2 million square feet, has more than 80 restaurants, an amusement park, a seven-acre water park, an NHL-size ice arena, submarines, an exact replica of the Santa Maria ship, a lagoon featuring special aquatic attractions, aquarium facilities, a miniature golf course, 26 movie theaters, a hotel, and a casino. And, of course, parking for 20,000 cars.

ESCAPE TO PARADISE

Until the beginning of the fifth century, the Venetian Lagoon was more of an escape hatch than anything else. As the Roman Empire began to crumble, people began to move to the Lagoon from the Italian mainland to escape the constant danger of invaders, especially Attila the Hun. Though tradition has it that Venice—which is actually 118 tiny islands connected by both bridges and canals—was founded as a city in 421 C.E., people continued to return to their cities and former lives until about 450 C.E. It became clear to them at last that life in the sanctuary of the canals was not only safer, but in fact quite pleasurable as well.

◆

The JAPAN Sherlock Holmes Club is the largest of the 375 such organizations worldwide, with 1,200 members.

BEFORE "FORE!"

No doubt that Scotland is the birthplace of golf—this compact-sized country, with more than 400 courses for five million inhabitants, is truly heaven on earth for the linksman. But the word *golf* did not stem from "Gentlemen Only, Ladies Forbidden!" as the old acronymal anecdote goes—most likely the name is derived from an Old Dutch word *kolf* or *kolve*, meaning club. Scottish dialect eventually transformed it into *gouf* or gowf.

Exactly when golf began to be played, however, is an even bigger mystery. Oddly, the first recorded mention of the sport, in 1457, was when King James II banned play, demanding that "fute-ball and golfe be utterly cryed down and not to be used." In 1502, this ban was repealed by King James IV of Scotland (1473–1513), a most learned monarch, who also practiced dentistry, founded the Royal College of Surgeons in Scotland, and introduced compulsory education. He became the first recorded golfer as we know it, playing on the North Inch (which still has a golf course today), and around Scone Palace, to the North of Perth.

As for the number of holes: on May 5, 1858, new rules were issued by the Royal and Ancient Golf Club at St. Andrews, Scotland. Among these was the stipulation that "one round of the links or eighteen holes is reckoned a match." At that time the course at St. Andrews happened to have eighteen holes, and that became the standard for golf courses around the world.

◆

INDONESIA is unique among all other countries, having a landmass composed completely of islands—17,508 of them—only 6,000 of which are inhabited.

WORLD'S LARGEST SUBWAY SYSTEMS
By annual ridership

City	Date Completed	Ridership Annually	Length (km)
Moscow	1935	3.3 billion	340
Tokyo	1927	2.6 billion	281+
Seoul	1974	2.2 billion	278+
Mexico City	1969	1.4 billion	202
New York City	1904	1.4 billion	371
Paris	1900	1.2 billion	211
London	1863	970 million	415
Osaka	1933	957 million	114
St. Petersburg	1955	821 million	110
Hong Kong	1979	786 million	82

Source: 2002 statistics, www.infoplease.com

THE THING FROM OUTER SPACE

The world's largest meteorite is located in Namibia, South Africa, and can be found on the Hoba farm near Grootfontein. It was discovered and first described by J. Brits in 1920 and weighs approximately 60 tons. Scientists estimate that the Hoba fell to Earth approximately 80,000 years ago. It is composed of 82% iron, 16% nickel, and 1% cobalt, as well as various trace elements.

◆

The WORLD'S current population growth rate is about 1.3 percent, with a doubling time of 54 years. The greatest recorded growth rate to date was in the 1960s at 2 percent, with a doubling time of 35 years.

WORLD JEWISH POPULATION
Countries with 100,000 or more Jewish residents:

United States	5,800,000
Israel	4,847,000
France	600,000
Russia	550,000
Ukraine	400,000
Canada	360,000
United Kingdom	300,000
Argentina	250,000
Brazil	130,000
South Africa	106,000
Australia	100,000

◆

From the 1920s to the 1960s, BURMA-SHAVE signs were as much a part of the American landscape as diners and gas stations. At the height of their popularity, there were 7,000 of them on the road, in every state except Arizona, Nevada, Massachusetts, and New Mexico; traffic was so sparse in these states at the peak of Burma-Shave Nation that the company didn't bother to post them there.

◆

CHINA is the country with the largest population: about 1.306 billion people. At the other end of the spectrum is The Vatican, the country with the world's smallest population, which hovers somewhere between 900 and 1,000 residents.

AN INSTRUMENT FOR WHERE

Although a rudimentary compass most likely appeared in China during the Han Dynasty (second century B.C.E. to the second century C.E.), it was not a navigational tool, but more of a divinational device for use in the art of feng shui. These first versions used a piece of lodestone floating on water, which pointed south. A flat piece of iron was then used as a pointer, eventually replaced by a needle; needles were magnetized by stroking them with a lodestone.

Magnetic compasses of a very simple kind were in use in the Mediterranean as early as the twelfth century, although little was known about how they worked. (Its evolution was so slow, in fact, that for some time superstitious sea captains believed if their crew ate onions, it would influence the compass's magnetism.) The compass is the first instrument to play a large part in modern scientific observation; the sundial and the wind vane were all that preceded it. The journeys of famous Chinese navigator, Zheng He (1371–1435), were the first recorded instances of the use of the compass as a navigational aid.

PLAY THAT PLUCKY MUSIC

Though it has long been held that the banjo is the only musical instrument indigenous to the United States, it is more likely that the earliest banjos were introduced in countries that were engaged in the slave trade. It is quite possible that the Arabs brought the instrument to the West African Coast, and it was then carried into America along with the Negro slaves. Thomas Jefferson wrote of its introduction in his *Notes on the State of Virginia* (1781), *"The instrument . . . is the banjar, which they brought hither from Africa."*

THE MAKING OF A FOXHOLE

Choose a piece of flat land, away from a water source.

For foxhole depth, measure height of soldier plus 6 to 8 inches, adding a few inches if foxhole is going to be covered.

If foxhole will be used for some duration, procure chicken wire, string, and stakes.

Put the chicken wire around the inner diameter of foxhole and tie it.

Place the stakes into the center of the parapet encircling foxhole, tying the top of the chicken wire to the stakes.

The firestep is where a soldier stands when in firing position. Off the step, there should still be sufficient room to receive head-level protection.

The water sump is located at one end of the emplacement to collect water.

The grenade sump is a small tunnel about 18 inches long, sloped downward at an angle of about 30 degrees, and is dug at the lowest level away from the firing position. Hand grenades thrown into the emplacement are disposed of here, and the fragments absorbed by the surrounding soil.

Excavated soil around the foxhole forms the parapet and is piled 3 feet wide and 6 inches high. This provides an elbow rest and extra protection from small arms fire.

A foxhole can be effectively camouflaged with available branches and foliage. Simple frames, with ponchos when available, create overhead cover.

RIDING THE RITZY RAILS

*If the idea appeals to you, and you are not afraid to
embark on a 2,000-kilometer journey powered only by steam,
we would be happy to have you join us .... We are leaving
Paris on Tuesday, 10th October, and we will be in
Vienna Wednesday night.*

Announcements like the one in the advertisement above
inaugurated the newest way to travel for wealthier Europeans
in 1883—and soon the Orient Express became the most fash-
ionable way to go. Though the train's original route was from
Paris through Munich, Vienna, and Sophia to Constantinople
(Istanbul)—1,980 miles—passengers could continue the
journey, traveling by boat across the Bosphorus to the Hay-
darpasa Railway Station to join the Taurus Express to Baghdad.

In the 1980s investors had many of the original cars
refurbished and reintroduced the Orient Express, running
from Paris to Vienna (864 miles) and from Stuttgart to Prague
(779 miles). American Orient Express also presently offers ten
deluxe train tours, ranging from National Parks of the West to
an Antebellum South Train Holiday. Agatha Christie has yet
to make a reservation.

HOW NOW HOCKEY?

Though there's some question as to how and where ice
hockey came to be, most agree that its beginnings lie in
Canada. One popular theory has the sport originating around
1800 in Windsor at Canada's first college, King's College
School, when the students began to play hurley, a field game,
on nearby skating ponds. A new winter version, "ice hurley,"
developed, which eventually became ice hockey.

STARRY SKIES

A *zodiac*, from the Greek for animal, is an imaginary band in the heavens extending approximately 8 degrees on either side of the apparent path of the sun, moon, and planets. It is divided into twelve parts of 30 degrees each—astrological signs each named for a constellation.

The Twelve Zodiacal Constellations
Aquarius, the Water-Bearer
Aries, the Ram
Cancer, the Crab
Capricorn, the Goat
Gemini, the Twins
Leo, the Lion
Libra, the Scales
Pisces, the Fishes
Sagittarius, the Archer
Scorpio, the Scorpion
Taurus, the Bull
Virgo, the Virgin

Twenty-nine Constellations North of the Zodiac
Andromeda, the Chained Lady
Aquila, the Eagle
Auriga, the Charioteer
Bootes, the Wagoner
Camelopardalis, the Camelopard (Giraffe)
Canes Venatici, the Hunting Dog
Cassiopeia, the Lady in the Chair
Cepheus, the King
Coma Berenices, Berenice's Hair
Corona Borealis, the Northern Crown

Cygnus, the Swan
Delphinus, the Dolphin
Draco, the Dragon
Equuleus, the Colt
Hercules (Kneeling)
Lacerta, the Lizard
Leo Minor, the Lesser Lion
Lynx, the Lynx
Lyra, the Lyre or Harp
Ophiuchus, the Serpent Holder
Pegasus, the Winged Horse
Perseus, the Hero (with Medusa's head)
Sagitta, the Arrow
Scutum, the Shield
Serpens, the Serpent
Triangulum, the Triangle
Ursa Major, the Greater Bear
Ursa Minor, the Lesser Bear
Vulpecula, the Fox (and the Goose)

Forty-nine Constellations South of the Zodiac
Antila, (Pneumatica), the Air Pump
Apus (Avis Indica), Bird of Paradise
Ara, the Altar
Caelum (Sculptorium), the Engraver's Tool
Canis Major, the Greater Dog
Canis Minor, the Lesser Dog
Carina, the Keel (Argo Navis)
Centaurus, the Centaur
Cetus, the Whale
Chamaeleon, the Chameleon
Circinus, the Pair of Compasses
Columba (Noachi), (Noah's) Dove

Corona Australis, the Southern Crown
Corvus, the Crow
Crater, the Bowl
Crux Australis, the Southern Cross
Dorado (Xiphias), the Gilthead or Swordfish
Eridanus, the River Po
Fornax (Chemicae), the Chemist's Furnace
Grus, the Crane
Horologium, the Clock
Hydra, the Water Serpent (feminine)
Hydrus, the Water Snake or Sea Serpent (masculine)
Indus, the Indian
Lepus, the Hare
Lupus, the Wolf
Pyxis Nautica, the Compass
Mensa (Mons Mensae), the Table Mountain
Microscopium, the Microscope
Monoceros, the Unicorn
Musca (Apis), the Fly or Bee
Norma, the Square or Rule
Octans, the Octant
Orion, the Hunter
Pavo, the Peacock
Phoenix, the Fabulous Bird
Pictor (Equuleus Pictorius), the Painter's Easel or Little Horse
Piscis Austrinus, the Southern Fish
Puppis, the Stern (Argo Navis)
Pyxis (Nautica), the Ship's Compass
Reticulum, the Reticule or Net
Sculptor (Apparatus Sculptorius), the Sculptor's Tool
Sextans, the Sextant
Telescopium, the Telescope
Triangulum Australe, the Southern Triangle

Tucana, the Toucan
Vela, the Sails (Argo Navis)
Volans, the Flying Fish

Asterisms are recognizable patterns of stars that have names, but are not constellations. These include the Big Dipper, which lies within the Ursa Major constellation; the Little Dipper; the Sickle, which forms Leo's mane; the Great Square, or Baseball Diamond, within Pegasus's body; and the Circlet, which lies within Pisces

◆

CHEERS!

Brewing is perhaps the most ancient manufacturing art known to man, though its exact origin remains uncertain. Records from 6,000 years ago show evidence that the Sumerians discovered fermentation, though perhaps by chance. The Chinese were brewing a beer called *kui* 5,000 years ago, and seven hundred years later, clay tablets of the Babylonians were found with beer recipes, citing brewing as a highly respected profession—one in which the master brewers were women.

BROADCAST NEWS

South Dakota may have Mount Rushmore, but that's nothing compared to what Blanchard, North Dakota, has to offer: the largest man-made structure in the world. It's the KVLY-TV tower, and at 2,063 feet high, the steel structure is taller than the Great Pyramid at Giza, the Eiffel Tower, and the Washington Monument combined.

"HELLO, SANTA?"
Important phone numbers at the North Pole*

Recorded local events
(907) 456-INFO

Federal Aviation Administration
(907) 474-0137
or (800) 992-7433

Highway and Travel Conditions
(907) 456-7623
or (800) 478-7675

Time & Temperature
(907) 488-1111

Weather
Recorded Weather (907) 458-3745
Forecast (800) 472-0391

* *North Pole, Alaska*

◆

C'MON-A MY HOUSE

Levittown, Pennsylvania, was the largest planned community
constructed by a single builder in the United States. Begun in
1951 under the direction of Abraham Levitt and his sons,
William and Alfred, the development occupied over 5,500
acres in lower Bucks County by the time it was completed in
1958, and included churches, schools, swimming pools, and
shopping centers. And, of course, 17,311 single-family homes.

ROMAN CATACOMBS

Though it has long been rumored that the catacombs were used extensively as hiding places for Christians from invaders of Rome, this is a fallacy: When Peter and Paul preached to early Christians, pagan and Jewish catacombs already existed. As burial places, they were considered sacred and protected by Roman law.

As a rule, a stairway leads below ground to a depth of about 30 to 50 feet; from this point diverge the galleries, which are from 10 to 13 feet in height, and seldom broader than necessary for two gravediggers, one behind the other, to carry a bier. In the side walls of the galleries horizontal tiers of graves are cut out of the rock from floor to ceiling. The number of graves in the Roman catacombs is estimated at two million. Burial continued in the catacombs until 410 c.e.

Over time, landslides and vegetation hid the entrances to the other catacombs, so that all traces of their existence were lost until 1578, when they were rediscovered. One of the most famous sites, the Crypt of the Popes, is in the Catacombs of Saint Callixtus and was discovered in 1854 by archaeologist Gian Battista de Rossi. Nine of the Catholic Church's early pontiffs were buried there:

St. Pontianus (230–235)
St. Antherus (235–236)
St. Fabian (236–250)
St. Lucius (253–254)
St. Stephen (254–257)
St. Sixtus II (257–258)
St. Dionysius (259–268)
St. Felix (269–274)
St. Eutichian (275–283)

WORLD-CLASS FOOD
The 50 best places on earth to dine

1. The Fat Duck, Bray, Berkshire, UK
2. El Bulli, Montjoi, Spain
3. French Laundry, Yountville, CA
4. Tetsuya's, Sydney
5. Restaurant Gordon Ramsay, Royal Hospital Road, London
6. Pierre Gagnaire, Rue Balzac, Paris
7. Per Se, New York
8. Tom Aikens, London
9. Jean Georges, New York
10. St. John, London
11. Michel Bras, Laguiole, France
12. Le Louis XV, Monaco
13. Chez Panisse, California
14. Charlie Trotter, Chicago
15. Gramercy Tavern, New York
16. Guy Savoy, Rue Troyon, Paris
17. Restaurant Alain Ducasse, Paris
18. The Gallery at Sketch, London
19. The Waterside Inn, Bray
20. Nobu, Park Lane, London
21. Restaurante Arzak, San Sebastian, Spain
22. El Raco de Can Fabes, San Celoni, Spain
23. Chessino dal 1887, Rome
24. Le Meurice, Paris
25. L'Hotel de Ville, Crissier, Switzerland
26. L'Arpege, Paris
27. Angela Hartnett at the Connaught, London
28. Le Manoir Aux Quat' Saisons, Oxford
29. Le Cinq, Paris, France
30. Hakkasan, London

31. Cal Pep, Barcelona
32. Masa, New York
33. Flower Drum, Melbourne
34. WD50, New York
35. Le Quartier Francais, Franschhoek, South Africa
36. Spice Market, New York
37. Auberge de Auberge de l'Ill, Illhauseern-Alsace, France
38. Manresa, California
39. Restaurant Dieter Muller, Bergisch Gladbach, Germany
40. La Masion Troisgros, Roanne, France
41. The Wolseley, London
42. Rockpool, Sydney
43. Yauatcha, London
44. The Ivy, London
45. Gambero Rosso, San Vincenzo, Italy
46. The Cliff, St. James, Barbados
47. Le Gavroche, London
48. Enoteca Pinchiorri, Florence, Italy
49. Felix, The Peninsula, Hong Kong
50. La Tupina, Bordeaux, France

Source: Restaurant Magazine, 2005

BY ANY OTHER NAME

The Bermuda Triangle—if you believe in it at all—is said to cover 440,000 square miles of ocean, with its points on the Bermuda Islands; Miami, Florida; and San Juan, Puerto Rico. It's also known as Devil's Triangle, Hoodoo Sea, Triangle of Death, and Jinx.

◆

VENUS is the only planet in the solar system that rotates clockwise.

WHAT A WAY TO GO

It was bound to happen: Since 1997, more than 150 people have been "buried" in space. Though seemingly a contradiction in terms, "space burial" is now available for the dearly departed—or at least part of them. A small amount (about 7 grams) of cremains can be placed in a lipstick-sized capsule and launched into space.

Some funerary missions are sent far enough only to orbit the Earth, finally reentering the Earth's atmosphere when the capsule slows down and burns up like a shooting star. The first space burial returned from orbit after only five years: it was launched on April 21, 1997, carrying the remains of twenty-four people, including *Star Trek* creator and science fiction writer Gene Roddenberry, and LSD proponent and guru Timothy Leary. The rocket circled Earth every ninety-six minutes, finally reentering in 2002 northeast of Australia. Future missions promise voyages to Jupiter and deep space—and though they leave our planet only intermittently, the price is currently an affordable $1,000—as long as you don't mind traveling with a few new friends.

Roddenberry's intergalactic presence is more extensive than most peoples': He has both a crater on Mars and an asteroid, 4659 Roddenberry, named after him.

PLAYING AROUND

The oldest board game in the world still being played is Go, which originated in ancient China more than 2,000 years ago; archaeologists have found a porcelain playing board from the Western Han Dynasty (206 B.C.E.–24 C.E.). The name for the strategic game-for-two is roughly translated from the Chinese as "Board Game of Surrounding One's Opponent."

MEETING MARY JANE

We can't really say whether they inhaled, but these countries have reported that more than 5 percent of their teenage and adult population has had at least one experience smoking marijuana:

Rank	Country	Percentage
1.	New Zealand	22.23
2.	Australia	17.93
3.	United States	12.30
4.	United Kingdom	9.00
5.	Switzerland	8.50
6.	Ireland	7.91
7.	Spain	7.58
8.	Canada	7.41
9.	Netherlands	5.24
10.	Belgium	5.01

THRILL ON THE HILL

"Blueberry Hill" was not first sung by "Fats" Domino but Gene Autry, in the 1940 western, *The Singing Hill*. Lyricist Larry Stock recalled that one important music publisher turned it down, saying "blueberries don't grow on hills," contrary to Stock's memories. A very wrong, very sorry music publisher, as it turned out—"Blueberry Hill" became a #1 hit.

◆

The estimated weight of the planet EARTH is 6,000,000,000,000,000,000,000 metric tons—or six sextillion.

WAY TO GO

War heroes, life-or-death messengers, newspaper reporters—
for centuries, "homers" have gone where and when others
could not go. Homing pigeons, also called rock doves, are
domesticated pigeons, *Columba livia*. There are reports that
during the Olympic games of 776 B.C.E., they carried news of
the winners to the different city-states of Greece, and were
used by the Egyptian pharaohs to relay news as far back as
2900 B.C.E.

Homers are bred to be able to find their way back home
over extremely long distances; this is relatively easy, as they
instinctively return to their own nests, food, and the mates
they have chosen for life. "Rookies"—birds less than a year
old—are trained to fly between one hundred and three
hundred miles a day, so that they can eventually join the "old
birds," who can easily fly six hundred or more miles a day.
Before a trip, homing pigeons are fed like marathon racers on a
special diet of high-protein grain mixture with extra carbo-
hydrates. Motivated by food, water, and the prospect of
returning to the nest, they will fly at speeds of forty to sixty
miles per hour.

Recently, researchers at Oxford University completed a
ten-year study on the birds and how it is they know their routes.
When learning a route for the first time, or on a long-distance
trip, homing pigeons use their own, mysterious navigational
system. But when they're taking a trip they're used to, they do
what humans do—go the way they know. GPS satellites used in
the Oxford study found the birds actually flying above major
highways, turning at stop lights, even circling roundabouts and
adding extra mileage—just because it's the route they recog-
nize, and it is mentally easier for them.

There is, by the way, a celebrity in the world of homing

pigeons in one Cher Ami, a World War I flying ace who was awarded the French Croix de Guerre for heroic service, delivering a dozen top secret messages—once despite being shot in the line of duty.

ON THE ROCK
What Life Is Like on the Rock of Gibraltar

0 percent arable land
0 percent permanent crops
0 oil production
More than ten thousand cell phones for a country that is eleven times the size of . . . the Washington Mall
1 television station
1 AM and 5 FM radio stations
18 miles of highway
7.5 miles of coastline

GROUND WORK

The Bingham Canyon Copper Mine in Utah is the biggest man-made hole on Earth. It is three-quarters of a mile deep and 2½ miles across. It has a couple of additional superlatives to its credit: Not only has it produced more copper than any other mine in history—about 17 million tons of the metal—but it bears the nickname of the "Richest Hole on Earth."

WHEN YOU HAVE TO GO . . .

Leave it to the Swiss: Travel experts say that the world's best rest stop is on highway M-1 in Deitingen. The bathroom, designed by architect Heinz Eisler, is cleaned every hour on the hour, without fail.

EMPIRE STATEMENTS

It is probably the most famous building in the world; it has twice been the tallest building in New York City (before and after the World Trade Center); it is the lead character in hit movies (*An Affair to Remember* and *Sleepless in Seattle*, to name two); an Irish governor broke ground for it on St. Patrick's Day; and it now shows streaming video of all it surveys, twenty-four hours a day, seven days a week, on its ESB TowerCAMS/TowerVISION.

So there are a lot of reasons to love the Empire State Building—but perhaps the most delightful is the lights atop the building, which are a daily looking glass into New York City life. Their colors honor national holidays, seasons, myriad ethnic groups living in the area, and worthy causes. Occasionally during spring and fall bird migration seasons and on cloudy or foggy nights, the lights are turned off. The first light shone on Election Day 1932 to let everyone within fifty miles know that Franklin Delano Roosevelt had been elected president. After special lighting for the 1964 World's Fair, the country's bicentennial, and the Yankees winning the World Series in 1977, a more permanent setup was designed in 1984. At this time, designer Douglas Leigh constructed an elaborate system of automated, fluorescent, color-changing apparatus in the uppermost mooring mast, which can be changed by just flipping a switch. And though the day's lighting extravaganza shuts off every night at midnight, Leigh also added thirty-two high-pressure sodium-vapor lights of just seventy watts each above the 103rd floor that create a golden "halo" effect around the top of the mast from dusk to dawn—a little nightlight for the city that never sleeps.

Here are just some of the reasons the Tower Lights celebrate (colors are listed from bottom to top):

Colors	Special Significance
Black/Green/Gold	Jamaica Independence
Black/Red/Yellow	German Reunification Day
Blue	Child Abuse Prevention Muscular Dystrophy Police Memorial Day
Blue/Blue/Red	Equal Parents Day
Blue/Blue/White	Colon Cancer Awareness Greek Independence
Blue/White/Blue	Americans with Disabilities First Night of Hanukkah Israel Independence Day Juvenile Diabetes Awareness Last Night of Hanukkah Tartan Day/Scotland
Blue/White/Red	Bastille Day
Blue/White/White	United Nations Day
Blue/Yellow/Black	Bahamas Independence
Gold	Oscar Week in New York City
Green	March of Dimes Organ Donor Awareness St. Patrick's Day
Green/Blue/Blue	Earth Day
Green/Green/White	Pakistan Independence
Green/Red/White	Wales/St. David's Day

Colors	Special Significance
Green/White/Orange	India Independence
Green/White/Red	Anniversary of Mexico's Independence
Green/Yellow/Blue	Brazil Independence
Lavender/Lavender/White	Stonewall Anniversary
No Lights	"Day without Art/Night without Lights" AIDS Awareness National Day of Mourning
Orange/Blue/Blue	New York Knicks Opening Day
Orange/Orange/Blue	Celebrate New York City New York City Marathon
Orange/Orange/White	Netherlands' Queens Day Walk to End Domestic Violence
Orange/White/Green	India Independence
Pink/Pink/White	Breast Cancer Awareness Month Race for the Cure
Purple/Purple/Gold	Westminster Dog Show
Purple/Purple/White	Alzheimer's Awareness Alzheimers' "Walk to Remember"
Purple/Teal/White	National Osteoporosis Society
Red	"Go Red for Women" Big Apple Circus Big Apple Fest/NYC&Co. Diabetes Awareness

Colors	Special Significance
Red	Fire Department Memorial Day Multiple Sclerosis Society Red Hot Summer Charity Event Valentine's Day
Red/Black/Green	Dr. Martin Luther King Jr., Day
Red/Blue/Blue	Haitian Culture Awareness
Red/Blue/White	New York Rangers
Red/Blue/Yellow	Colombia Independence Philippines/Manila Day
Red/Gold/Green	Grenada Independence
Red/Gold/Red	Lunar New Year
Red/Red/Green	Holiday Season
Red/Red/White	Pulaski Day Red Cross Month Swiss National Day
Red/Red/Yellow	Autumn Colors Ringling Bros. and Barnum & Bailey Circus
Red/White/Blue	Armed Forces Day Election Day Flag Day Fleet Week/Memorial Day Independence Day Labor Day Presidents' Day Veterans Day

Colors	Special Significance
Red/White/Green	Feast of San Gennaro Columbus Day
Red/White/Red	Peru Independence Poison Prevention Month
Red/White/White	Leukemia and Lymphoma "Light the Night"
Red/Yellow/Green	Portuguese Independence
White	ESB Lighting
White/Blue/Blue	Jackie Robinson Day
White/Red/Red	Qatar Independence
Yellow	Broadway on Broadway U.S. Open
Yellow/Blue/Blue	Ukrainian Independence
Yellow/Orange/Yellow	Corporate Philanthropy Day
Yellow/White/Yellow	Spring/Easter

For several months after the events of September 11, 2001, the Empire State Building lights glowed red, white, and blue twenty-four hours a day at the request of the men and women working at the World Trade Center site.

◆

A SNOOD, an ornamental net in the shape of a bag, confines a woman's hair on the nape of the neck.

BOOK STORE

Though its original purpose was to serve as the research arm of the U.S. Congress, the Library of Congress has grown to be the largest library in the world. It holds more than 130 million items, which require more than 530 miles of shelving. The collections include more than

- 29 million books and other printed materials
- 2.7 million recordings
- 12 million photographs
- 4.8 million maps
- 58 million manuscripts

THAT REINDEER SONG

Where did Rudolph come from? There were "eight tiny reindeer"—and Rudolph was *not* one of them. So how did Rudolph get to be part of Santa Claus's Christmas Eve crew?

Rudolph the Red-Nosed Reindeer was born in 1939 in Chicago, Illinois, and before he went to work for Santa, he held a job at the Montgomery Ward Department Store. During Christmas seasons in the past, the store had bought coloring books for kids; this year they decided to save some money and write and produce a story of their own. Store copywriter Robert L. May got to work, and 2.4 million books were given away that season; by 1946, 6 million children knew the story of Rudolph, thanks to the giveaway. Eventually May's brother-in-law, songwriter Johnny Marks, developed the music and lyrics to the famous song, and in 1949 Gene Autry, of "Singing Cowboy" fame, recorded it, selling 2 million copies the very first year.

ROUTES TO FREEDOM

Its existence was an open secret, but from its inception, the routes and locations that made up the Underground Railroad remained one of the best-kept secrets of American history. Its mission—to help Southern American slaves escape to freedom in the North or Canada—was of such import, and was fraught with such grave consequences, that even today the actual routes American slaves traveled are generally a matter of speculation, or remnants of oral history.

The Underground Railroad was more a loose association of people rather than an actual mode of transportation or even a systematic route of escape. Reports as early as the 1700s tell of slaves escaping, but by the passage of the Fugitive Slave Bill of 1850, it became considerably more dangerous for runaway slaves to stay in urban areas in the North. Therefore, more slaves—there are reports of more than thirty thousand—continued on to Canada, or fled south to the Caribbean. Earlier in the nineteenth century, organized flights through Pennsylvania and New Jersey were aided by Quaker abolitionists. At its height between 1810 and 1850, nearly one hundred thousand people escaped enslavement via the Underground Railroad, a fraction of the estimated 4 million slaves who would eventually escape. Historians do know that flights to freedom took place mostly at night on routes more well known and easy to travel, such as the Mississippi River; the Appalachian Mountains; from Washington, D.C., to Frederick County, Maryland; and to ports such as New Bedford, Massachusetts, where the labor-hungry whaling industry assured that men of color would disappear virtually overnight for sea voyages of several years.

Perhaps the most amazing and yet little-known aspect of the Underground Railroad has come to light only in the last few decades. Folkloric reports and oral history tell of sympathizers in homes both north and south of the Mason-Dixon Line who aided the refugee slaves with a series of signals given by the placement of quilts in and around their homes. According to some, both the patterns of the quilts and the way and place in which they were hung directed the travelers to the next safe haven along the route.

COUNTRIES WITH LESS THAN ONE PERCENT UNEMPLOYMENT*

Andorra	0.00	Isle of Man	0.60
Norfolk Island	0.00	Uzbekistan	0.60
Guernsey	0.50	Jersey	0.90
Aruba	0.60		

*CIA World Factbook 2005.

HOLD ON TO YOUR HAT

On the planet Jupiter, winds regularly whip around at an average of 225 miles per hour. But Saturn is by far the windiest planet, though photos taken in the 1980s vary greatly with more recent pictures sent back from the Hubble Space Telescope from 1996 to 2002, which indicate that winds have slowed by about 40 percent at Saturn's equator. Where wind speeds formerly peaked at 1,000 miles per hour, now 600 miles per hour is the norm.

But Earth can't really compare: The highest surface winds ever recorded on this planet are said to have been a gust of 231 miles per hour, clocked on New Hampshire's Mount Washington on April 12, 1934, and tornado winds of 318 miles per hour measured during a 1999 tornado in Oklahoma.

THE GREATEST SHOW ON EARTH

It may seem that a form of entertainment so simple would be many thousands of years old—but the circus is quite a modern event. Though the way the circus is constructed and the way the audiences assemble are reminiscent of ancient Roman amphitheaters and coliseums, those ancient venues were used as racecourses or devoted to gladiatorial combat.

Entertainment display that took to the road has existed since some man found out he had a talent others did not, but the modern circus was created in 1768 by Philip Astley (1742–1814). Originally the owner of a horseback-riding school in London, Astley used a circular performance ring for two reasons: It was easier for the riders to balance on a moving horse, and an audience could see everything. The trick-riding display soon grew to include clowns, acrobats, jugglers, musicians, tumblers, tightrope walkers, and dancing dogs, and what we know as the circus was born. Astley's circus was so popular that soon he opened another in Paris, and other performers with their various acts followed suit around the world.

Astley's original space was sixty-two feet in diameter, and later he made it smaller, forty-two feet, which became an international standard for circuses. It wasn't until 1825 that American J. Purdy Brown began putting the circus under a tent. Brown realized that most large American cities lacked buildings a traveling show could move into and out of for short periods of time. At first the tents weren't exactly "big tops"— they were very small, containing only one ring and a few hundred seats. At the height of their popularity, however, circuses exhibited simultaneously in two rings (1872) and then three (1881), and the great American tented circuses became the stuff of legend.

"THE 400"

It was socialite Ward McAllister who said there were only about four hundred people in New York who were at ease in a ballroom. So in the late 1880s, he and Caroline Schermerhorn Astor went so far as to make a list. To be more exact, to be included in "Mrs. Astor's Four Hundred," one had to be from a family who had money, and for three generations, one's ancestors could not have worked in the trades. Reports are that Mrs. Astor's parties were apparently quite dull.

SILVER SERVICE

Everyone knows where the gold is: Fort Knox, Kentucky, is the home of the U.S. gold depository. There are nearly 150 million ounces there today, worth about $60 billion—pretty hefty for a storage facility constructed in 1936 of granite, steel, and concrete at a cost of only $560,000. (It sounds insecure, but rest assured: The vault door alone weighs more than twenty tons—and no one person is entrusted with the entire combination.)

But since 1939 there's been a little-known silver depository as well—in West Point, New York. The "Fort Knox of Silver," as it's nicknamed, is actually the West Point Bullion Depository. It presently houses both silver and gold, and it is even used occasionally as a mint. In the 1970s, a severe shortage of pennies (if one can even imagine such a thing) moved the government to produce "mintmarkless" one-cent coins at West Point, and over the years the depository has also manufactured gold and silver commemorative coins, and American Eagle Bullion coins in proof and uncirculated condition. In 2000, it struck the first-ever gold and platinum bimetallic coin.

IF YOU BELIEVE . . .

Who ghost there? If the spirit world is a place as real to you as your own home, you know that ghosts make their homes all over the world, and in the strangest places . . .

The *azeman* is a ghostly woman who haunts the villages of Surinam in South America. The unwelcome phantom bites a piece of flesh from the big toe of sleeping persons, sapping their blood.

Canada has many haunted sites, a recent example being the Firkins' House in Heritage Park in Fort Edmonton, Alberta. Many claim that it is haunted by the presence of Dr. Firkins' son, upset that the house itself was moved to a new site. Tour guides have been pushed while going down the stairs, visitors report the smell of lilacs, and some hear singing in one of the bedrooms.

The posh ocean liner *Queen Mary I* may have retired to Long Beach, California, in 1967, but some say she hasn't exactly settled down. Since the ship's doors opened as a museum and hotel, there have been several ghostly sightings, including one near a doorway marked number 13, where a young crewman was crushed to death during a 1966 safety drill.

The City Cemetery in Port-au-Prince, Haiti, is haunted by ghastly apparitions of decomposing bodies.

In Brisbane, Australia, ghosts are quite political: They're found in the Old Government House, the Parliament House, and especially City Hall, where at least three ghosts haunt the hallways. One is an elegant woman in period clothes seen on the main staircase, the second a maintenance man who rides the elevator that killed him as he installed it in the 1930s. The last is an American sailor in the Red Cross Tea Room, stabbed to death by another sailor over a young Australian woman.

A ghost has been walking along the battlements of the Cape Town Castle in South Africa for more than three hundred years. The tall, luminous figure disappears over the edge at the approach of a human.

South Africa's Port Elizabeth Highway (between the Hex River Mountains and Drakensberg) is haunted by a phantom automobile that is blamed for several accidents.

Asia considers Singapore its most haunted city. Strange lights are not uncommon, and people are slapped by an unseen presence at the Changi Beach Houses. Specters also beg for food along the coast near Lor Halus—one spot even has a spirit that calls for help and then runs away.

Security cameras at the Parliament House in Suva, Fiji, recorded their ghost for five minutes. The footage was so clear that it was shown on national television, and the prime minister is said to have called for an exorcism.

Mount Everest claims to have its own spirit in climber Andrew Irvine, who died there in 1924. His ghost shares tents with climbers and encourages them to make the final ascent. First reported by climbers Dougal Haston and Doug Scott in 1975, he has been seen several times since.

There is an angry specter in Tasmania—a settler from England who hanged himself over a broken heart. He spent three years building a new house for his wife-to-be back home; when he sailed back to wed her, he found that she had gotten lonely and married another. Grief-stricken, he returned to Australia and killed himself in the courtyard of the house he had prepared for his love. Even today, cattle and horses become unnerved around the house called Garth, and the cries of the Englishman are still often heard.

Ghosts are so pesky in Iceland that there used to be a law that enabled people to legally summon to court a ghost that had been tormenting them, and have it bound over to authorities.

In Germany, the White Lady of Hohenzollerns is more mobile than most. She visits castles all over Germany, including Neuhaus, Berlin, Bechin, Tretzen, and Raumleau. Believers say she is Princess Perchta von Rosenberg, who haunts descendents of her cruel husband.

Austrian Baroness Russlein von Altebar seeks her revenge against any descendants of Count Johannes Rathenau, who slaughtered her family during the Middle Ages. She first appears as a beautiful courtesan before turning into a rotting corpse. In Vienna, she once boarded the cab of Walther Rathenau, who immediately died of fright. One Major Helmut Rathenau met much the same demise.

Russians are not at all surprised to have ghosts in their homes. In fact, they're so common that they have classifications. *Domovoi* are domestic ghosts that tend to be nuisances or poltergeists, but help with chores if treated with respect. *Domovikha* are quiet, but their presence can be sensed in certain rooms.

Scottish lore stars the *bean-nighe*, an ugly Scottish banshee that shows up to wash the blood from the clothes of those who are about to die. Picture this for scary: one nostril, one big, protruding tooth, webbed feet, and long, hanging breasts.

In England, the ghosts go straight to the top: 10 Downing Street. The resident phantom there is a man dressed in Regency-style clothes who appears in several rooms. Speculation is that he may be a former prime minister, especially as he appears only during a national crisis.

WHENCE THE WEB?

The World Wide Web is so ephemeral, so beyond most people's ken, that it's hard to believe that it started in a *place*. But it did. Tim Berners-Lee (the son of two people who met designing a computer) designed it alone, in 1989, while he was working at CERN (the European Organization for Nuclear Research) in Switzerland. Basically, Berners-Lee took everything on the Internet and wove it into a web. The very first Web site, by the way, was nxoc01.cern.ch, and the very first Web page was http://nxoc01.cer n.ch/hypertext/WWW/TheProject.html.

◆

JUST A HOLE IN THE GROUND

About 150 meteor collision sites have been identified on Earth. Ten of the largest visible craters—by their diameters—are:

Meteor Crater, Arizona: 4,150 feet
Wolf Creek, Australia: 2,789 feet
Henbury, Australia: 722 feet
Boxhole, Australia: 574 feet
Odessa, Texas: 558 feet
Tswainga, South Africa: 433 feet
Wabar, Saudi Arabia: 381 feet
Oesel, Estonia: 328 feet
Campo del Cielo, Argentina: 246 feet
Dalgaranga, Australia: 230 feet

"HAPPINESS NET"

Don't be so sure you can't quantify happiness. This survey shows the countries that lead in what's called "Happiness Net." Samples of various populations were questioned as to how happy they were—very happy, quite happy, not very happy or not at all happy. The net was determined by taking the percentage of the first two (the happy people) and subtracting the percentage of the last two (the unhappy people). Maybe it's the politics, the scenery, or just the way of life, but in general it looks like if you're not happy, it's time to move north.

Rank	Country	Happiness Net
1.	Iceland	94%
2.	Netherlands	91%
3.	Sweden	91%
4.	Denmark	91%
5.	Australia	90%
6.	Switzerland	89%
7.	Ireland	89%
8.	Norway	88%
9.	Venezuela	87%
10.	United Kingdom	87%
11.	Belgium	86%
12.	Philippines	85%
13.	United States	84%
14.	France	84%
15.	Finland	83%
16.	Austria	81%
17.	Canada	75%
18.	Poland	74%

19.	Japan	72%
20.	Turkey	71%
21.	Bangladesh	70%
22.	Spain	68%
23.	Italy	64%
24.	Uruguay	60%
25.	Argentina	59%

Source: Nationmaster.com

TRULY THE "SHOW ME" STATE

Though its true and exact location may forever remain a mystery, most scientists and historians believe that the Garden of Eden—if it existed at all—lay somewhere in what was Mesopotamia, between the Tigris and Euphrates rivers. There are followers of Joseph Smith, founder of the Church of Jesus Christ of Latter-Day Saints, who say Smith came upon a mountaintop, surveyed all below him, and declared that Missouri was indeed the original Garden of Eden.

"THE GREAT INDIAN WAY"

One old Algonquin Indian trade route lasted throughout the centuries and became perhaps one of the most successful streets of commerce in history. It was originally called the Wiechquaekeck Trail. Today, people simply call it Broadway.

The GREAT CHICAGO FIRE gets all the attention, but a more destructive fire took place the same day, October 8, 1871, in Peshtigo, Wisconsin.

AKA

Some people—and some places—have big ideas about themselves. All around the world, places give themselves nicknames, and not too surprisingly, they're often self-aggrandizing. How many places can actually *be* "The Garden Capital of the World," after all? But very often these nicknames are an insight to culture, agriculture, history, pride, geography, and humor. Here are some secret personalities from around the world:

Aberdeen, Scotland	The Granite City
Albany, Georgia	Good Life City
Albany, Oregon	Home of the Timber Carnival
Alexandria, Egypt	Pearl of the Mediterranean
Alpine, Texas	Gateway to the Big Bend
Annapolis, Maryland	Crabtown
Atlanta, Georgia	The City Too Busy to Hate
Auckland, New Zealand	City of Sails
Baltimore, Maryland	Charm City
Banaras, India	Luminous City
Bandon, Oregon	Storm Capital of the World
Bangkok, Thailand	Venice of the East
Bardstown, Kentucky	Bourbon Capital of the World
Beaver, Oklahoma	Cow Chip Throwing Capital of the World
Bemidji, Minnesota	Home of Paul Bunyan and Babe, the Blue Ox
Berrien Springs, Michigan	Christmas Pickle Capital of the World
Bickleton, Washington	Bluebird Capital of the World
Birmingham, Alabama	Pittsburgh of the South
Boston, Massachusetts	The Cradle of Liberty

Bristol, Tennessee	Food City
Bucharest, Romania	The Little Paris
Budapest, Hungary	The Pearl of the Danube
Buffalo, New York	The City of Good Neighbors
Burlington, Iowa	Loader/Backhoe Capital of the World
Butte, Montana	Copper City
Byron, Ohio	The Fountain City
Calgary, Alberta, Canada	The Stampede City
Cape Girardeau, Missouri	Rose City
Cape Hatteras, North Carolina	The Graveyard of the Atlantic
Castroville, California	Artichoke Center of the World
Charleston, South Carolina	Palmetto City
Chicago, Illinois	Hog Butcher to the World
Christchurch, New Zealand	The Garden City
Cincinnati, Ohio	Queen City
Cleveland, Ohio	Mistake on the Lake
Cody, Wyoming	Rodeo Capital of the World
Columbus, Ohio	The Crossroads of Ohio
Coober Pedy, Australia	Opal Capital of the World
Cooperstown, New York	Birthplace of Baseball
Council Bluffs, Iowa	Iowa's Leading Edge
Cozad, Nebraska	Alfalfa Capital of the World
Cuernavaca, Morelos, Mexico	The City of Eternal Spring
Dallas, Texas	Big D
Dayton, Ohio	Birthplace of Aviation
Detroit, Michigan	Motown
Dipolog City, Philippines	Orchid City
Douglas, Wyoming	Jackalope Capital of the World
Drumheller, Albert, Canada	Dinosaur Capital of the World
Durham, North Carolina	City of Medicine
Edinburgh, Scotland	Athens of the North

Erie, Pennsylvania	The Gem
Fallbrook, California	Avocado Capital of the World
Florence, Italy	The City of Lilies
Fort Myers, Florida	The City of Palms
Franklin County, Virginia	Moonshine Capital of the World
Frannie, Wyoming	Biggest Little Town in Wyoming
Gainesville, Florida	Hogtown
Gallup, New Mexico	Drunk Driving Capital of America
Gilroy, California	Garlic Capital of the World
Gotland, Sweden	Pearl of the Baltic
Grants Pass, Oregon	Where the Rogue River Runs
Greenfield, California	Broccoli Capital of the World
Hammondsport, New York	Cradle of Aviation
Hammonton, New Jersey	Blueberry Capital of the World
Hatch, New Mexico	Chili Capital of the World
Hershey, Pennsylvania	Chocolate Town, USA
Hollywood, California	Tinseltown
Holtville, California	Carrot Capital of the World
Hong Kong, China	Pearl of the Orient
Hood River, Oregon	Windsurfing Capital of the World
Hoople, North Dakota	Tater Town
Houston, Texas	Magnolia City
Indianapolis, Indiana	Circle City
Indio, California	Date Capital of the World
International Falls, Minnesota	The Icebox of the United States
Isleton, California	Crawdad Town, USA
Jackson, Mississippi	Chimneyville

Jerusalem, Israel	City of David
Kalamazoo, Michigan	Celery City
Kansas City, Kansas	Heart of America
Kokomo, Indiana	City of Firsts
Keizer, Oregon	Iris Capital of the World
Lacrosse, Wisconsin	Barbed Wire Capital of the World
Laramie, Wyoming	Gem City of the Plains
Letchworth, England	The First Garden City in the World
Lodi, California	The [Tokay] Grape Capital of the World
London, Ontario, Canada	The Forest City
Los Angeles, California	The Big Orange
Louisville, Kentucky	City of Beautiful Churches
Lowell, Wyoming	The Rose City of Wyoming
Madison, Wisconsin	Four Lake City
Manila, Philippines	Pearl of the Orient
Mar del Plata, Argentina	Queen of the Coast
Marysville, California	Gateway to the Gold Fields
Mattoon, Illinois	Bagel Capital of the World
Medellin, Colombia	Orchid City
Meeteetse, Wyoming	Where Chiefs Meet
Memphis, Tennessee	Bluff City
Miami, Florida	Little Cuba
Milwaukee, Wisconsin	Cream City
Minneapolis, Minnesota	Flour City
Mobile, Alabama	City of Five Flags
Montreal, Quebec, Canada	The City of Saints
Mountain Iron, Minnesota	Taconite Capital of the World
Mountain View, Arkansas	Folk Music Capital of the World

Moyobamba, Peru	Orchid City
Nashville, Tennessee	Music City, USA
Newark, New Jersey	Brick City
New Haven, Connecticut	Elm City
New Orleans, Louisiana	The Crescent City
New York, New York	Gotham
Oakdale, California	Cowboy Capital of the World
Oroville, California	City of Gold
Oxford, England	City of Dreaming Spires
Palatka, Florida	Bass Capital of the World
Paris, France	City of Light
Pasadena, California	City of Roses
Patterson, California	Apricot Capital of the World
Pearsonville, California	Hubcap Capital of the World
Petaluma, California	Egg Basket of the World
Philadelphia, Pennsylvania	Rebel Capital
Pittsburgh, Pennsylvania	Steel City
Placerville, California	Hangtown
Portland, Maine	Forest City
Prague, Czech Republic	The Golden City
Providence, Rhode Island	Beehive of Industry
Quebec City, Quebec, Canada	The Gibraltar of North America
Queenstown, New Zealand	Extreme Sports Capital of the World
Reno, Nevada	The Biggest Little City in the World
Rigby, Idaho	Birthplace of TV
Rochester, New York	Snapshot City
Rockport, Massachusetts	The Mendocino of the East
Rome, Italy	The Eternal City
Rye, New York	Border Town

Sacramento, California	River City
St. Louis, Missouri	Gateway to the West
St. Petersburg, Russia	Venice of the North
Salem, Massachusetts	City of Witches
San Antonio, Texas	Alamo City
San Diego, California	America's Finest City
North San Jose, California	The Golden Triangle
Santa Fe, New Mexico	The City Different
Santa Rosa, New Mexico	The SCUBA Diving Capital of New Mexico
Saratoga Springs, New York	Spa City
Savannah, Georgia	Garden City
Sault Ste. Marie, Michigan	The SOO
Seattle, Washington	The Emerald City
Selma, California	Raisin Capital of the World
Shah Alam, Malaysia	Orchid City
Sonora, California	The Queen of the Southern Mines
Stockholm, Sweden	Venice of the North
Stockton, California	California's Sunrise Seaport
Sturgis, Michigan	Curtain Rod Capital of the World
Syracuse, New York	Salt City
Taxco, Mexico	Silver Capital of the World
Thousand Oaks, California	T.O.
Tijuana, Mexico	Television Capital of the World
Toledo, Ohio	Corn City
Toronto, Ontario, Canada	Hogtown
Tulelake, California	Horseradish Capital of the World
Umeå, Sweden	Björkarnas Stad (The City of the Birches)

Vancouver, British Columbia, Canada	Gastown
Venice, Italy	Bride of the Sea
Värnersborg, Sweden	Lilla Paris (Little Paris)
Västerås, Gurkstan	The Cucumber City
Vicksburg, Mississippi	The Gibraltar of America
Victoria, Australia	The Cabbage Patch
Victoria, British Columbia, Canada	Little England
Walla Walla, Washington	The Town So Nice They Named It Twice
Washington, D.C.	Capital City
Waterbury, Connecticut	Brass City
Waynesboro, Georgia	Bird Dog Capital of the World
Wenatchee, Washington	Apple Capital of the World
West Hollywood, California	Boystown
Wheeling, West Virginia	Nail City
Wichita, Kansas	Emerald City
Windsor, Ontario	Tijuana North
Yates Center, Kansas	Hay Capital of the World

◆

COLLEGE HONORS

Landmark College takes the honors as the most expensive college in the world. This specialized institution, located in Putney, Vermont, is an accredited college that caters to students with learning disabilities such as dyslexia and attention deficit hyperactivity disorder.

122